Wills and probate

a Consumer Publication

Consumers' Association
publishers of **Which?**
14 Buckingham Street
London WC2N 6DS

a Consumer Publication

edited by Edith Rudinger

published by Consumers' Association
publishers of **Which?**

Consumer publications
are available from
Consumers' Association
and from booksellers.
Details are given at
the end of this book

© Consumers' Association March 1983

ISBN 0 85202 251 4
and   0 340 33165 8

Photoset by Paston Press, Norwich
Printed in England

contents

foreword

Death is a subject people do not like to think about. Many people defer, until it is too late, deciding what is to happen to their possessions when they die, and making a will.

This book is intended to help at two separate stages, which in any individual case should be separated by a decent interval.

Firstly, it explains how to make a will in a simple case, including a description of what not to do, what to include and how the will must be signed and witnessed. Secondly, the book describes the administration by the executors of the estate of someone who has died. Here, too, only a straightforward case is described, but this is done in some detail, to give the full picture. What happens when there is no will is also explained.

The probate registry provides special machinery to deal with laymen who wish to act as personal representatives without having a solicitor. This book supplements this by explaining, in detail, not only the probate registry procedure but also what goes before and what comes after.

This book is not concerned with complicated tax saving or tax avoidance issues but, at certain points, circumstances appropriate for straightforward or substantial savings of tax are mentioned, particularly where tax can be saved by a fairly simple course of action. In many cases, however, the details of these schemes would involve the drawing of documents such as discretionary settlements or deeds of variation of an estate; to implement such schemes, you would need to get the professional advice of a lawyer, accountant or other financial advisor. The tax savings would be greater than the cost involved.

This book explains the law and procedure in England and Wales; it does not cover what happens in Northern Ireland or in Scotland.

making a will

Some people have an unconscious fear of making a will, as if to do so were to take a positive step towards the grave. Others, when asked if they have made a will, smile nervously and say that they have so little to leave that it would not be worth the trouble. But the total value of a person's property is not much of a factor in considering this. A man might have only £250, but his circumstances could make it essential that he should leave a will, to prevent his property going to the crown. His neighbour might have £100,000 and yet not need to make a will in order to have his wishes fulfilled.

intestacy

The property of a person who dies without leaving a valid will – dying intestate, the law calls it – is divided among his family according to rules in the Administration of Estates Act, which applies to anyone whose domicile at the time of his death is in England or Wales, even if he died elsewhere. (Domicile is what a person regards as his permanent home, irrespective of where he actually happens to be living at any particular time.)

Where his possessions are worth under £40,000, all goes to his widow. Where it is more than that, the position becomes more complicated. The widow gets the furniture, the car and the rest of the personal effects of her late husband, together with the first £40,000 out of the rest: stocks, shares, insurance policies, bank accounts, the house and so on. What is then left is divided into two halves. One half goes to the children equally, there and then. As to the other half, the widow gets a life interest in it: an income consisting of dividends from shares, rent from houses, and so on, for the rest of her life. On her death, the property comprising the half-share from which she has been receiving the income is then divided equally among the children, just as the first half was earlier on.

If no wife survives, the whole estate is divided between the children equally. If there is a wife, but no children, she gets everything up to £85,000 and half the rest. The other half of the rest goes to the parents of the man who died.

On a wife's death intestate, her property is divided in the same way as a husband's.

The property of an unmarried man without children who dies intestate is divided between his parents; if they are dead, his brothers and sisters share it; if he has none, his grandparents share it; and if they are dead, aunts and uncles share the estate. The children of an eligible relative who has already died generally receive the share which their parent would have received. If a bachelor dies without any descendants of his grandparents alive to inherit his property, his estate goes to the crown, if he has made no will.

On the death of an unmarried woman who dies intestate, her property is divided in the same way as a bachelor's or childless widower's.

None of the property of a man or woman who is divorced goes to the ex-spouse, under the intestacy rules.

no need to make a will?

These are the intestacy rules in outline. They are described in greater detail at the end of this book. If you wish your property to be divided according to the rules just described, there is no pressing need for you to make a will, as your wishes will probably be met by the automatic operation of the intestacy rules.

why it is useful to make a will

But there are advantages in making a will, even so. Firstly, you may become better (or worse) off as the years go by, and while the intestacy rules may suit your present financial position, they may not be appropriate in a few years' time.

Also, you have to take account of inflation and the fall in the value of money. If your property, excluding the personal effects, comes to more than £40,000 so that your widow will get a life interest, she may be all right at first, according to current values and rates of interest. But the value of the house may take up most of the £40,000, leaving very little capital on which she has a life interest. She may survive you for many years, and she may find that what was at first a perfectly adequate income for her to live on has depreciated to a pittance.

Where there is an intestacy, there are restrictions on what sort of investments can be used for the widow's life interest (she cannot touch the capital, of course, apart from the first £40,000, as she is only entitled to the income). But if you make a will, you can remove these restrictions and so give her a chance to have a better income.

You may also have to consider the possibility of a husband and wife being killed together in an accident, leaving young children behind. Were this to happen, the property of both would be held on trust till the children came of age. In the meantime it would have to be invested, and the restrictions on the kind of investments that can be selected may prevent the property being dealt with as flexibly and advantageously for the benefit of the children as might have been wished. Making a will could give greater freedom regarding investments, and the children could be better off. Apart from saying what is to happen to property, a will can be used to express a number of other provisions and wishes. Even where some of them may not be binding on the people concerned, it is a useful way of recording your views.

One matter often included in a will is the appointment of one or two people, well respected and trusted, to act as guardian for any infant children. This, in a will, can help to give you peace of mind.

If you have left no will, the nearest relatives are the ones primarily entitled to take on managing your estate (that is the property you leave behind) and be what are called the administrators. If you make a will, however, you can choose who shall take on this task. In this case, those appointed to act are called executors. If, therefore, your preference is to have someone who is not a near relative to administer your estate – a friend, say, or your solicitor – you need to make a will.

All in all, therefore, it is better to make a will, even if the intestacy rules would dispose of your property as you would wish.

do-it-yourself?

There is no legal requirement that a will should be drawn up or witnessed by a solicitor and quite a lot of people do in fact make their own. But there is one thing worse than not making a will at all: making a mess of making a will. Lawyers say that they make more money out of home-made wills than they do out of drawing up wills for clients.

There is probably some truth in this. People who prepare and sign their own will can go wrong in one or more ways and, after their death, there could be long and expensive court cases to get the trouble sorted out. A will is a technical legal document. Problems can arise about whether it was signed and witnessed properly and about the exact meaning of what it says. It is not surprising, therefore, that laymen sometimes go astray when they embark on will-making unaided.

It is not a good idea to use a printed form bought in a stationer's shop and to make your will by filling in the blanks and signing according to the directions. The form may be misleading, or at least it may not give effect to your precise intentions, and by striving to make the wording of your will fit the framework of the form, you may inadvertently commit some blunder. It is better to avoid forms altogether, and instead to write the whole thing out from scratch.

when to use a solicitor

A solicitor is likely to charge anything from £30 to £100 for preparing a will in a normal case, depending on the circumstances. (Do not hesitate to ask beforehand how much you are likely to be charged.) Sometimes a solicitor is essential. If, for example, a person is receiving an income from a family trust under which he has the right to determine, by his will, who should benefit from the trust property on his death, the will by which he does this should be prepared by a solicitor to deal with the matter properly. Also, if the permanent home of a person making a will is in a foreign country, or some other foreign element is involved, a solicitor should be consulted.

No matter how simple the circumstances, a larger estate is more likely to benefit from legal advice, especially when it comes to questions of tax planning so as to save capital transfer tax (CTT). Smaller estates can also benefit from good advice. But the smaller your estate is going to be, the less likely it is that there is scope for sidestepping the Inland Revenue.

A solicitor should also be consulted where your assets include a business or a farm, shares in a family private company, or items of a peculiar character; likewise, where you are separated, but not divorced, from your wife or husband, and in any case where you intend to cut your spouse or your children out of your will or where you wish to state people who should benefit from your property in succession (that is, one after the other, known as 'life interests') rather than making an outright gift to one person.

It is only, in fact, where your affairs are straightforward that you should contemplate making a will without going to a solicitor. Anything unusual in your financial or family situation should be regarded as a reason for not making a will by yourself.

formalities for making a will

You must be of age, that is at least 18 years old, to make a will. The legal formalities for making a will apply to any person whose permanent home is in England or Wales. Scottish law about wills is somewhat different. The situation in Northern Ireland is nearly the same as in England and Wales.

The most important part of your will is obviously the part which states how you wish your property to be divided when you die. Before starting to write the will itself, you should have given careful consideration to this. Jot down on a piece of paper what you think you are worth, all told. Knock off your debts, including mortgages. Consider what changes are likely to take place in your total wealth in the next five years or so, and take those changes into account in estimating your wealth and possessions. Make a list of all the people whom you wish to benefit. Then you can decide how to divide up your property. You may want to leave specific items of property to some people: your wedding ring to your granddaughter, for example, or the piano to your musical nephew. Then you may wish to give money to a few of your relations and friends: £100 to the child of an old friend, or £25 to the boy next door. You may wish to leave the same sum to each of a number of your relations: '£500 to each of my brothers and sisters living at my death' would be suitable. Or you could, if you like, divide a larger sum between a class of relations: '£2,000 to be divided equally between all my grandchildren living at my death'. But there are some dangers in describing people in your will as a class, rather than naming them individually. Does the word children include adopted and illegitimate children, for instance? Are a husband's brother's sons covered by the word nephews? Are the husbands of aunts included in the word uncles, or does it mean brothers of parents only? To avoid any difficulties of that kind, it is better to list them all with their names.

gift to a charity
Some people wish to leave money to a charity, and there is generally no problem about this (and gifts to charity are usually exempt from capital transfer tax). It is usually sufficient to say: 'I give £200 to the Imperial Cancer Research Fund'. Sometimes these words are added: '. . . and the receipt of the secretary or treasurer, or other person professing to be the proper officer for the time being, shall be a sufficient discharge to my executors'. This is for the protection of the executors and beneficiaries: if the executors get such a receipt, there cannot then be any question that they have paid the money to the wrong people, nor could the other beneficiaries be made to pay back anything to the estate.

It is important to get the name right and, particularly in the case of a small or less well-known charity, to add an address or sufficient other information so that the charity can be properly identified. It is a good idea to get in touch with the charity and find out what is its official title. Is Oxfam the right name to use in a will, for instance? Is it sufficient just to write 'Dr Barnado's'? A charity will probably be glad to be asked about this, because getting its name right in your will may make the difference between getting the money or not, when the time comes. While in contact with them on this point, you should ask them whether they want to suggest any particular form of words in a will under which they are to receive a legacy. If they do, you may as well adopt the clause they suggest.

other gifts

Then you have to decide who is to inherit the rest of your property. How you dispose of your property is up to you, but there are several points you should consider. For instance, if you leave property on trust for your wife for life, she cannot touch that capital and only gets the income while she is alive.

When considering giving specific items in your will, remember that a will speaks from death, that is, it will apply to your personal situation at the time of your death, not at the time you make the will. If, for example, after making a will but before you die, you sell the item of jewellery you left to your goddaughter, she will get nothing. Because of this, you may wish to provide that, if this should happen, another item should be substituted for it.

It is not practical to give away everything in stated bits so as to dispose of the lot of it exactly. Even if you could make the necessary calculation in relation to your current wealth – '£150 to cousin George, and £3,427.68 to my brother Sidney' for instance – it would not apply next month, when you will be that much richer or poorer, and certainly not next year, or the year after. So what you do is this: after disposing of specified items and sums of money, you give the remainder – the residue, lawyers call it – to some named person, who thus inherits the residue of your estate, whatever it turns out to be. You could, of course, provide that your residue should be divided, in whatever proportions you like, among a number of people.

Furthermore, you could provide that the residue should be invested, and only the income paid to someone (your wife, perhaps during her life), the money itself to be divided between other people (your children, perhaps) on the death of the person entitled to the income for life (that is, the life tenant). This means that the property will on that person's death devolve in accordance with your own will and not under the will of (or intestacy relating to) the life tenant's estate, which would have been the case had the property been given outright. This can be important where, for instance, you want to keep property in your family rather than allowing it to pass to your wife's family. If property were given to her absolutely and she died, after you, intestate and you had no children who survive her, the property would pass to her parents or other members of her family under the intestacy rules, or it could pass to anyone else if she made a will. By the life interest method, your wife still benefits from the property during her life, but the property carries on in accordance with your will when she dies.

trying to disinherit a dependant

Most people naturally favour the members of their own immediate family, and this is a notion which the law encourages, for you are not entirely free to dispose of your property as you like. If for any reason you decide that your wife, husband, or any of your children or anyone financially dependent on you should inherit little or nothing under your will, any of them might apply to the executors, or to the court, after your death, for reasonable provision to be made for them out of what you left. Those who can apply for some provision to be made are: the surviving husband or wife; former wife or husband who has not remarried; sons or daughters, including step-children, and anyone who was being maintained by you before you died. Any idea you may have of disinheriting a spouse or child is therefore liable to be frustrated.

There are circumstances where such people can properly be excluded from benefitting from your estate, but to ensure that the best wording for this is used in your will, you should take professional advice in such circumstances.

CTT

Capital transfer tax, currently the only form of death duty, depends on the total value of the estate, and also takes account of gifts made during life. A person can state in the will whether any gift should bear its own tax (that means that the recipient has to pay it), or be free of tax (that means that the tax is paid out of the residue). Tax on property other than land and buildings is generally paid out of the residue, so that the beneficiaries who receive stocks and shares, or sums of money, get their inheritance in full. But in the case of houses and land, the beneficiary normally bears an appropriate proportion of the duty. The will can, however, specifically provide that the CTT, even on a house, should be paid out of the residue. This is done by saying, for example, 'I leave my house, 22 Pridham Place, to my nephew Fred Redhill, free of tax'; your wishes in this respect should in all cases be stated explicitly.

In most cases it is not necessary, in making a will, to calculate by how much the residue will be reduced by CTT, funeral expenses and legal costs, because the residue will constitute the great bulk of your estate anyway. If your estate will be greatly depleted by the gifts of individual items (the specific bequests) and the gifts of stated sums of money (the pecuniary legacies), you have to remember that it is, in effect, the residuary legatee who generally has to pay the CTT, the funeral expenses and the legal costs of administration, and so could end up with little or no benefit from your estate. So, you may prefer to state that the other beneficiaries should bear the appropriate proportion of CTT.

executors

Before starting to write the will itself, you must decide who are to be your executors. It is by no means a mere formality to be an executor: there can be a good deal of work and a great deal of responsibility involved in this task. It would be unfair to inflict this job on someone who would have preferred not to be appointed. A person cannot be compelled to act as an executor if he really does not want to, but it can happen that a person feels he ought to accept, having been appointed, even though he would have declined if given the chance when the will was being drawn up. So, find out in advance whether a person you have in mind to be your executor is willing to be appointed. If he is not, appoint somebody else.

Whom should you appoint? In normal circumstances, a husband will appoint his wife to be an executor, and vice versa, especially where they do not have grown-up children. This is a good idea as a rule, because the wife is probably the residuary legatee. It is sensible that the person who has the biggest stake in the estate should have a hand in its administration. It is perhaps as well, though, that a wife should not have to shoulder this burden alone. She will have enough to cope with at the time of her husband's death without this, so it is often a good idea to appoint another executor to act with her. A grown-up son or daughter would be an obvious choice. If you have grown-up children, you may prefer to appoint them without appointing your wife, if only to transfer the work and responsibility into their hands.

In simple cases, one executor is quite sufficient. It is common to appoint two, however, and this is a good idea where the burden needs to be shared, and is virtually essential where the will would set up a trust – for example, for children. A close friend of the family is sometimes a suitable choice for co-executor with the surviving spouse, or perhaps a near relation who is used to dealing with business affairs. When someone not in the immediate family circle is appointed as executor, it is sometimes thought suitable to leave him a legacy – £250 say – for undertaking the office of executor.

It is common to appoint a solicitor to be an executor; in this case, the solicitor will include a clause in your will enabling him to charge normal professional fees for his legal work in administering the estate. Without a charging clause, as it is called, he would not be entitled to a fee. His charge for preparing the will may be nominal, perhaps only £5. He knows that he will have the advantage of dealing with the legal side of administering the estate in due course.

appointing a bank

A bank can act as the executor of your will, and quite a lot of people appoint a bank to do this job. There are certainly situations where a bank is the most suitable choice. One is where there is family strife to such an extent that any executor appointed from within the family is likely to cause discontent. Also, a bank may be the best choice where the main beneficiary cannot be the executor for some reason, and there is no other suitable individual at hand; this could happen, for instance, where a widow is making a will in favour of her young children. An advantage of appointing a bank is that it can claim to be experienced in questions of investment and of trust management generally, and this might be useful. A bank can be a good choice where the will creates trusts which are likely to continue for many years; for example, a trust giving your widow the income from your estate for the rest of her life – a life interest, in fact. Here, one advantage of having a bank is that it goes on for ever, whereas mortal trustees will need replacement sooner or later, which can be a bother and an expense.

Like all promotional material issued by commercial organisations, the bank's literature about executorship should be looked at carefully to see what it omits. It is unlikely to point out the disadvantages.

The Public Trustee is a government department which can be appointed to be your executor, as can some trust corporations. These all operate in much the same way as a bank acting as executor, and charge for this service.

The main reason why people do not appoint a bank to be their executor is the cost. Banks do not work for nothing, and require to be paid for acting as executors. This is often a percentage of the net value of the estate itself, plus a percentage of the annual income, where a continuing trust is created by the will. On top of this, solicitors' fees for the probate work are likely to be charged.

All in all, it is probably better to appoint individuals to be your executors, if suitable candidates are willing to act. There are likely to be some tasks which require a personal touch: sorting out the personal belongings of the person who has died, for instance. Banks may employ competent and sympathetic staff, but they are no substitute for the right friend or relation.

However, an advantage of appointing a bank as your executor is that you can be pretty sure that it will survive you, no matter how long you live, whereas there is always some chance that an executor you appoint will die before you. For the same reason it is better to select younger rather than older people to be your executors. Even so, it is best to provide in your will for a substitute executor to act if one or other (or both) of those appointed should die before you, or not wish to act as your executor.

If you appoint a bank to be your executor, you should use the clause which the particular bank suggests for the purpose. The local bank manager can supply you with a copy of the words, and may ask to see a draft of the will.

beneficiary dying first

If a son or daughter of yours, destined to receive something under your will, were to die before you, but a child or grandchild of that son or daughter survives you, the gift you had left to the son or daughter will go to that son's or daughter's issue. Anyone else destined to receive something under your will who dies before you, will not inherit from you, nor will his or her children. In the case of a pecuniary legacy ('£100 to John Brown') or a specific bequest ('my diamond brooch to Jane Brown') no problem arises: the item will simply fall into residue, that is, swell the amount that will go to the person who is to receive the residue.

If the residuary legatee himself dies first, that would leave part of your property undisposed of; this is called a partial intestacy. For example, generally a husband gives the main part of his estate to his wife, so that the wife becomes the residuary legatee. But what if the wife were to die first? The husband could then make a fresh will, making provision for the children instead, or, if there are no children, disposing of it elsewhere according to the circumstance. But it might happen that husband and wife are both victims of the same road accident, the wife being killed outright and the husband surviving for a few days, but then dying without having a chance to make a new will. In such a case, the husband's will, leaving everything to his wife, would be largely abortive, because she would have died first.

What would then happen to the bulk of his property, which his will left her, follows the rules about intestacy. These might well not accord with his wishes, so that it would be better for the husband to make specific provision for this possibility in the will itself, by saying to whom his property should go if his wife does not survive him. In many cases, this would be the children. If they are under age, the will might well go on to deal with that situation in greater detail, for instance, to lift some of the restrictions which would otherwise limit the executors' powers of investing the property for the children's benefit, and similar matters. The executors might feel a bit hampered in running the trust which would arise for the children until they come of age, unless the will gave them a free hand to do what they think best. This could be done in a series of clauses which would only come into effect if the wife died first.

The matter can be taken a stage further. The wife may literally survive her husband, but only just. What if, in that terrible accident, the husband is the one who is killed outright, while the wife is seriously injured, goes into a coma and dies a week later? As she survived her husband, she inherited his property under his will (or under the intestacy rules), even though she may never have appreciated the fact. The husband's property, having passed to her in this way, would then be distributed according to her will. If she left no will, it might then pass to her relations if she has no children, and this could mean that all the husband's property goes to the wife's family. This can be dealt with by saying in the will that the wife is to receive the residue of the estate only if she survives the husband by at least 30 days. There is no magic in selecting 30 days, instead of 25 or 40, say. But if husband and wife die as a result of the same accident, it can arbitrarily be assumed to be unlikely that one would outlive the other by more than about 30 days.

If, therefore, this formula is adopted, the main provision in the will simply says: 'I give the rest of my property to my wife, if she survives me by 30 days'. Both possibilities are then covered in the simplest way: the expected course of events of the husband dying first, leaving his wife to survive him by several years at least; and the unexpected (but possible) course of events of the wife dying first, or of their both being killed as a result of the same accident.

what to say and how to say it

A will is chiefly concerned with disposing of property, but it can be used for some incidental matters as well. Perhaps the commonest of these, traditionally, is to specify the way in which you want your body to be disposed of: burial or cremation. You may want to leave your body to be used for medical research, your eyes for corneal grafting, or your kidneys for transplantation. If you want this, it is more important to let your nearest relative or the person you live with know than to put it in your will, and always to carry a 'multidonor bequest' card with you. The Consumer Publication *What do to when someone dies* gives details of what to do if you wish to donate a body for medical purposes.

appointing a guardian
Sometimes a guardian for young children is appointed in a will. This is particularly important when one parent of the children has already died. The guardian has the right to determine questions relating to the home, education and marriage of children under age. Where there are young children, it is advisable, in any event, to appoint a guardian (or two people to be joint guardians), in case both parents are killed together. Make it somebody in whom you have complete trust that he or she, or they, would bring up the children in the way you would wish. Make sure that whoever you wish to appoint is willing to do this.

what not to say

A will is not the place for philosophical reflection, nor for expressing love, gratitude, hate, despair or any feeling about the world in general, or anyone in particular. Your will, when you are dead, will be available for public inspection, and anyone will eventually be able to see it at Somerset House, and obtain a copy of it. You may not want your private thoughts to be open to the public gaze, and it could be a source of embarrassment to your relatives if you were to explain why you left nothing to your prodigal son, or to reaffirm your love for your wife.

You should not put down any outrageous thoughts or reasons for making particular gifts or failing to benefit, for example, a close relative: a will can be invalid if the testator is insane or even if it can be shown that he did not give proper consideration to those obligations he ought to have considered.

Express your wishes simply, without embellishment, explanation or apology. If you really want to make it clear why you have left your property as you have, it is probably better to do this in an ordinary letter which can be left with the will. It is always possible that if you were to go into unnecessary detail in the will itself, you might unwittingly affect the interpretation that would be put on the words. For example, if you were to say: 'I give £500 to my cousin Willie Bolter, confident that he will do what is right by the rest of my cousins', there may be a question of whether this created a binding legal trust in favour of the other cousins. It may be that this doubt could only be resolved by an expensive court case after your death. You should instead say either: 'I give £500 to my cousin Willie Bolter' and leave it at that, or: 'I give £500 to be divided equally between . . .'.

It is also inadvisable to say 'I leave £500 to Mr. and Mrs. Harry Green' because this does not make it clear whether they should receive £500 each or £250 each, nor what is to happen if one of them were to die before the testator.

say it simply and clearly
You should aim to be precise and clear in what you say in your will. Never assume that people know what you mean; they may not, and anyway the will can only be interpreted on the basis of the words you actually use.

It can happen that although a testator said one thing in his will, it is obvious that he meant something different. If this is so, the law may well stick to what he said, rather than what he meant, so strict are the rules of interpretation. Avoid legal terminology, even if you feel you know the correct legal meaning. It is perfectly possible to make a will in a normal case without using technical language. So, wherever it is possible, use an ordinary word and not a legal one. It is easy to cause havoc by choosing inappropriate legal expressions. Even lawyers sometimes come unstuck by doing this, and there is a strong case for cutting out a lot of the legal jargon they often employ in drawing wills for their clients. They use jargon partly from professional caution, resulting in a desire to use only expressions which have a tested legal meaning, or may do so partly from a desire to impress their clients. Laymen unaided should avoid legal language.

At the same time, choose your ordinary language with care. Beware of sloppy, loose expressions. If you were to say: 'I give all my money to my wife Clara', this might mean just the cash about the house, or it might mean all the cash plus what is in the bank, or it might mean everything you own. If you intend the latter, you should say: 'I give everything I own to my wife Clara'.

Sometimes found in a home-made will is a clause which reads like this: 'I leave everything to my wife Clara; and on her death it is to be shared between my sons Albert and Sidney'. This is a disaster, and likely to have an effect quite different from what the testator intended. The point is this: if he leaves everything to his wife Clara so that, on his death, his property becomes her property, his will cannot then go on to say what is to happen to her property on her death. That is a matter for her to deal with in making her will. She may or may not choose to leave it to the sons Albert and Sidney. If the husband leaves his property to his wife, he cannot ordain what is to happen to it after her death (or during her lifetime, for that matter). If he does say what is to happen to it, or what remains of it on her death, the chances are that this leaves his wife with a mere life interest; that is, the right to get just the income from the property for the rest of her life, with no right to touch the capital. Of course, a husband may intend to give his wife a life interest only, in which case he should say something like this: 'I give all my property to my trustees upon trust to sell it (but with the power to postone sale), to invest the proceeds and hold the investments on trust to pay the income to my wife Clara during her life, and on her death to divide them equally between my sons Albert and Sidney'. In such a case the widow, during the rest of her life, would have a life interest, and the two sons, during her life, would have a 'reversion' giving them the property on her death. But if the husband intends that his widow should be able to do what she likes with the capital, and does not intend to restrict her to having only a life interest, he should just say: 'I give everything I own to my wife Clara', and leave her to decide what is to happen to what remains of it by the time she dies.

revocation clause
A later will does not automatically revoke an earlier one. There is, therefore, one more clause which should always be included in a will. This says that any previous wills are revoked. Even though you have not in fact made a will before, it is a good idea to include a statement that previous wills are revoked. Without such a clause, your executors might wonder, after your death, whether perhaps you left any earlier wills. If a person leaves two wills, and they are not inconsistent with each other, they stand

together. It may save your relatives a pointless search for any earlier will if
you show that it is revoked anyway, and therefore no longer valid.

examples of wills

Here is an example of how a will may be prepared.

Matthew Seaton is in his thirties, is married and has two children, a boy
aged six and a girl aged four. He owns his house, but he has a mortgage on
it with a building society. He has an endowment insurance policy which will
produce about £8,000 in 22 years' time, or on death. He owns about £700
worth of shares which are quoted on the stock exchange. He has about £500
invested with a building society, and most of the furniture and effects in the
house belong to him, as well as the car. He has a bank account which is
seldom in credit to the tune of more than £150. His salary is £9,500 a year
and he hopes to be earning around £15,000 before he reaches his ceiling.
His employers run a contributory pension scheme under which he will get
a pension when he retires, and under which his wife Emma will receive a
pension on his death, and something extra for the children if he dies while
they are under 18.

Matthew is in good health and expects to live to a ripe old age. But like
anyone else, he may be dead by midnight tonight, so he is making a will.
The notes he makes on a scrap of paper (which he will be sure to destroy
once the will is made, in case they might be confused with the will itself)
might read like this:

What I own

(1)	House: 14 Twintree Avenue value: say	£45,000	
	Subject to mortgage to Forthright Building		
	Society; with still owing (about)	10,000	
	∴ net value of house to me		£35,000
(2)	Endowment: worth on my death		8,000
(3)	Various shares		700
(4)	Amersham Building Society		500
(5)	Furniture and effects in house: value as		
	for insurance, say		4,000
(6)	Car		1,100
(7)	Current account at bank, say		200
			£49,500
		Call it	£50,000

Notes for will

(1) Revoke previous wills
(2) Executors: Emma and brother David
    substitute for either of them: friend Andrew Shervington
(3) Guardians: Janet and Nicholas
(4) Cremation, eyes and organ transplant
(5) Bequests:
     (i) golf clubs to Donald
    (ii) cello to Daniel
   (iii) lawnmower to Rosemary Bruton
(6) Legacies:
     (i) £250 to David or Andrew, if they are my executors
    (ii) £60 to Leslie Roberts
   (iii) £100 to cancer research
(7) Residue to Emma
(8) If she dies before me, trusts for children with appropriate clauses.

Having carefully thought out how he would like to frame his will, Matthew turned his attention to the precise wording. He wrote it out in draft first.

When he was considering the substitute executor, he had to decide whether the substitution was to take effect if only one of the named executors did not, for any reason, prove his will (that is, obtain a grant of probate), or whether it should take effect only if both of those named did not prove his will. In a simple case, where there is no life interest and the property will go to people who are all over 18, it is common and more straightforward to have only one executor and so the substitution would only be necessary where neither of them proved the will. However, Matthew knew that it was possible that his children could inherit directly if Emma died first, and this could happen before they all reached 18. So he decided that the substitution was to operate if either of the executors did not prove.

He made a few amendments to tidy up the wording, and when he was quite satisfied with it, he typed out the will itself – the engrossment, as lawyers call it – on a large piece of paper. He could have written it out by hand, but typing is better, so that there can be no question of illegibility.

He decided that single spacing was the best way to type it, mainly because the whole will would then fit on to one sheet of paper, leaving sufficient room at the bottom for the signatures of himself and the witnesses. Apart from looking slightly absurd, there could be legal problems if the signatures appeared on a page by themselves. If a will extends to more than one side of a piece of paper, it is best to leave at least one full clause for the next page. Also, the continuation should be on the back of the first page rather than on a fresh sheet.

Matthew took some pains in typing out his will, and managed to avoid making any typing errors. This is quite important, because alterations appearing in a will are assumed (until the contrary is proved) to have been made after the will was signed, and so to form no part of it. If he had made any errors in preparing the engrossment, he and the witnesses would have had to authenticate the alterations by writing their initials in the margin alongside each alteration.

This is what he typed:

WILL of Matthew John Seaton
of 14 Twintree Avenue, Minford, Surrey

1. I revoke previous wills.
2. My wife Emma and my brother David Gordon Seaton are to be my executors, but if either does not prove my will, my friend Andrew Shervington is to be an executor instead.
3. I appoint Janet and Nicholas Saunders of 4 Field Close, Chesham to be guardians of my infant children after the death of my wife.
4. I wish my eyes and any other parts of my body to be used for medical purposes and my body to be cremated.

5. I give the following bequests:
   - (*a*) my golf clubs, bag and trolley to my nephew Donald Millington (16 Durham Terrace, Leeds);
   - (*b*) my cello to my son Daniel;
   - (*c*) my motor mower to my neighbour Mrs Rosemary Bruton.
6. I give the following legacies:
   - (*a*) £250 to my brother David if he is an executor who proves my will;
   - (*b*) £250 to my friend Andrew Shervington (5 Sandpit Drive, Minford) if he is an executor who proves my will;
   - (*c*) £60 to Leslie Roberts (36 Grove Park, Norwich);
   - (*d*) £100 to the Imperial Cancer Research Fund.
7. I give to my wife Emma the whole of the rest of my estate.
8. If my wife Emma does not survive me, the following shall apply:
   - (i) I give the whole of the rest of my estate to my executors as trustees. They are to sell everything not in the form of cash, but they may postpone the sale of anything as long as they like. After paying my debts, any taxes or duties payable on my death, and the expenses of my funeral and of administering my estate, they are to invest or apply what is left in any type of property, just as if it were their own money.

   - (ii) My trustees may give to the guardians of my children up to one third of what is left, to enable them to acquire a larger property if they need it for my children.
   - (iii) My trustees are to divide whatever is left of my estate (including any income from it) equally between those of my children who reach the age of 18, and may apply the actual assets rather than cash if they think fit, without requiring the consent of any other person.
   - (iv) If any child of mine predeceases me, or dies under the age of 18, leaving children who do reach that age, then those grandchildren of mine are to divide equally between them the share of my estate which their parent would have received if that parent had lived long enough.

     Date: ....
     Signature: ....
     Signed by Matthew John Seaton in our presence and then by us in his: ....
     ....

In that form, Matthew Seaton's will was ready to be signed. It would not all fit into the front side of the sheet of paper which Matthew was using, so he carried over to the back of the sheet, at the point where the will said (ii) My trustees may give to the guardians. . . .

The only part of it which was at all difficult was clause 8, the trust for the children if his wife did not survive him. There was always the possibility that he and his wife might die before their children had come of age. If this were to happen, it would not be possible for the trustees to pay out all the capital money until each child's 18th birthday, and until then the money would have to be held on trust for them.

more freedom of choice for trustees
Clause 8 (i) created what is known as a trust for sale; it is mainly intended to cover the position if there is a house, or other real property. The trustees are given a free hand to decide what should be sold and what should be kept. Even though the will says they are to sell everything, they need not, and can hand over any part of the estate – furniture, effects, shares, car, or anything else – to a beneficiary in settlement of the whole or part of any entitlement under the will. Where no consents are required for the handing over of actual assets rather than cash, stamp duty can be saved on the document of transfer. Stamp duty is payable on 'consideration' passing, or value given, and the Inland Revenue regards the giving of consent as a consideration, thus rendering the value of the transferred assets liable to stamp duty. Where no consent is required, no consideration passes, and therefore no stamp duty is payable.

The direction to sell is a legal device required when real property (houses, buildings or land) is left to people creating a life interest. To avoid complicated legal pitfalls, when real property becomes involved, it is prudent to include a 'trust for sale', using this form of words.

The trustees are also given a free hand concerning the investment of the property for the benefit of the children. Without these words in clause 8 (i), the executors – or trustees, as they will become once they have sorted out everything following Matthew's death – would be able to invest the property only in what are called trustee securities. These consist of stocks, shares and other investments which are so reliable that it would be unlikely that the trustees would lose the money. Only gilt-edged securities (those where payment is guaranteed by the government), the large building societies and public companies, and similar safe investments are included.

They tend not to be the kind which increase their capital value, however, so they are vulnerable to losing their real value through inflation.

If you prefer that these restrictions on the trustees' power to invest your property should apply in your case, you should leave out the words 'or apply' and all the words in clause 8 (i) after '. . . what is left'. But people often prefer to widen these legal powers of investment.

Some wills contain a clause setting out the sort of investments that may be used. If you have complete confidence in your trustees, you can do as Matthew has done: remove all restrictions on their power to invest your property. The word 'invest' would indicate that income-bearing assets must be bought. But adding the words 'or apply' allows the trustees to put the money into something which may not produce any income, so that land and houses may be bought, or low-yielding gilts, or gold sovereigns, or Krugerrands, in the hope of obtaining capital growth. You leave it to their judgement, trusting that they will take good advice from experts, to choose whatever is best. With this unlimited power to invest your property, they could, if they liked, put some of your money into some highly speculative venture, and lose it.

when there are young children
A guardian who suddenly finds himself in charge of young children may need a larger house to accommodate them. Clause 8 (ii) gives the necessary authority to the trustees to give the guardian a lump sum from your estate towards the cost of a larger house (plus extra furniture, perhaps). There is no obligation on the guardians to give back this money to the children when the guardianship comes to an end when the children reach the age of eighteen. The sum could be a lump sum (£5,000 say), or a percentage of the estate.

Clause 8 (iii) provides that the children are to share the estate equally. But this would depend on each one becoming 18. It is not essential to add this requirement, but it is commonly done. One reason is to guard against the fecklessness of youth. If one of your children, at 16, knew that he was entitled, come what may, to a share in an estate, he might blue the lot in advance on an orgy of spending. You guard against this to some extent by providing that he is not eligible for a share until he becomes 18. This makes it more difficult for him to raise a loan on the strength of his inheritance, for if he were to die between 16 and 18, say, his share would be worth nothing.

But though he may never in fact reach 18 and inherit, he can get a share in the income of the property, before he comes of age. The trustees can, if they like, use the income that is received from the investments to help meet the cost of maintaining and educating the children. Any income they do not use for this would be accumulated, invested, and ultimately distributed, with the capital of the estate, as each child becomes 18.

In 1970 the age of 18 was substituted for 21 as the age at which a young person comes of age. But a parent can stipulate any other age as the age at which his children shall receive his property. Matthew took the view that his children would be competent and ought to have access to the property at 18. Some parents feel that their children ought not to receive any property until they are 21, or even 25, and that much wiser. They feel the trustees are more competent at managing the investments. Even if you feel a child ought not to have the capital until 21 or even older, it is usual to allow the child to receive the income from the date he is of age. However, it is also possible to delay the payment of income to a child for up to a maximum period of 21 years from the date of a testator's death – but for this, professional advice should be sought.

Some of the capital of the estate can also be used to help with the maintenance or education of the children, while they are still minors. Up to half of each one's expected share in the capital can be used in this way. Take an example: imagine that Matthew Seaton is killed, with his wife Emma, in an accident, and that he leaves the residue of his estate worth £50,000 on trust for any of his children who reach the age of 18. When he made his will he had two children. At the time of his death he has four, aged 11, 9, 5 and 3. The £50,000 would be invested for them, and the income from it (£4,000 a year, if it produces 8 per cent) could be used for their maintenance and education. Each one would expect to receive whatever sum represented £12,500 when he or she reached 18. If any one of them died before that, his or her share would be divided between the surviving three equally. But in spite of the risk of this happening, it is still open to the trustees, if they want to, to use up to half of the capital (in this case, £6,250, assuming the fund retained a constant value) for helping with the maintenance or education of each one of them: half of each one's expected share. And if one of the children for whom that was done then died before his 18th birthday, and so never really got to the stage of inheriting his share, nevertheless no part of the advance made to him would have to be paid back to the others.

The hypothesis in clause 8 (iv) is that one at least of the children might die under the age of 18 (without having become absolutely entitled to his share), and yet have already had a child of his or her own: a grandchild of Matthew Seaton, in the example. Clause 8 (iv) provides that the grandchild inherits the share which, but for earlier death, his father (or mother) would have inherited on his (or her) 18th birthday. In relation to a child over 18 who died before his father, leaving children, it is likewise advisable to say that these grandchildren are to get their parent's share, and clause 8 (iv) does this. An age could have been specified at which the grandchildren were to become entitled but, unlike the rules relating to children, the age at which a grandchild will become entitled must be less than 21 years.

All this may seen very far removed from reality as Matthew is sitting down now, about to sign his will, with two healthy children noisily around him. His own death is sufficiently unthinkable. The death of one of his children leaving a baby grandchild behind is hardly to be contemplated. But it is sensible to provide for what may conceivably happen in the future.

The will was now ready for signature. Before considering the way to sign it, take some more examples of how to draw a will.

where there are no young children
Many people do not have young children to consider, and the comparatively complicated clause 8 in Matthew Seaton's will would, therefore, not need to appear at all. Quite often a person wishes to leave all his property to one other person, with no complications. A man whose children are grown up may wish to leave all his property to his wife. In his case, the simplest possible will would do (but there are CTT considerations to be borne in mind). It would also be suitable for an unmarried man or woman who wished to leave everything to one other adult, a brother or friend, perhaps. In that situation, the will merely needs to leave everything to the one person, and that person should be appointed to be the executor. It could read like this:

Will of Margaret Ellen Seaton, 12 Chiltern Court, Foden Gardens, Hastings, Sussex.
I revoke previous wills. I appoint my brother Matthew John Seaton of 14 Twintree Avenue, Minford, Surrey, to be the sole executor of this will, and leave to him everything I own.
Date: ....
Signature: ....
Signed by Margaret Ellen Seaton in our presence, and then by us in hers:
....
....
....

wife's or husband's will

A wife should make a will, just as much as a husband should. The amount a person has to leave is not particularly relevant to the question of whether he or she should make a will. Each should make a will.

Husband and wife sometimes make their wills together and at the same time. When this happens, they often make their wills complementary, the one being the mirror image of the other.

Let us suppose that Matthew Seaton's wife Emma made her will at the same time as he made his. It would read something like this:

Will of Emma Seaton of 14 Twintree Avenue, Minford, Surrey.

1. I revoke previous wills.
2. I appoint my husband Matthew John Seaton and my cousin Edward Seymour Forbes to be the executors of my will. If either does not prove my will, I appoint my brother-in-law David Gordon Seaton to be an executor instead.
3. I appoint Janet and Nicholas Saunders of 4 Field Close, Chesham, to be guardians of my infant children after the death of my husband.
4. I wish my body to be buried.
5. I give to my husband Matthew the whole of my property.
6. If my husband Matthew does not survive me, the following shall apply:
   (i) I give the whole of my estate to my executors as trustees. They are to sell everything not in the form of cash, but they may postpone the sale of anything as long as they like. After paying my debts, capital transfer tax, and the expenses of my funeral and of administering my estate, they are to invest or apply what is left in any type of property just as if it were their own money.
   (ii) My trustees may give to the guardians of my children up to one third of what is left, to enable them to acquire a larger property if they need it for my children.
   (iii) My trustees are to divide whatever is left of my estate, including any income from it, equally between those of my children who reach the age of 18 and may apply the actual assets rather than cash if they think fit without requiring the consent of any other person.

(iv) If any child of mine predeceases me, or dies under the age of 18, leaving children who do reach that age, then those grandchildren of mine are to divide equally between them the share of my estate which their parent would have received, if that parent had lived long enough.

Date: ....

Signature: ....

Signed by Emma Seaton in our presence, and then by us in hers:

....

....

She appoints someone on her side of the family – her cousin – to be an executor with her husband, She does not have to, and if there is any fear of antagonism between them, it is probably better to have someone who gets on with the husband. The substitute executor is, in this case, her husband's brother. She could easily have appointed Matthew to be sole executor, with a provision that her cousin and brother-in-law should be her executors if Matthew did not prove her will.

Where guardians are appointed, husband and wife should appoint the same people, to avoid any possible conflict. Guardianship would only arise after the death of both husband and wife.

capital transfer tax

Capital transfer tax (CTT) is the only form of duty or tax imposed on the death of a person who regarded his real and permanent home as being the UK. It is imposed, however, regardless of the country in which such a person was actually living at the date of his death, or where he died.

The general rule is that CTT is imposed on all the property which is transferred by reason of a person's death, whether that person owned the property outright or had only a life interest in such property. The tax is charged at progressively higher rates of tax on the value of a person's estate, that is, the property he leaves when he dies, and it is charged also on all gifts made by a person during his life. To find the point on the scale for the rate at which the tax is payable, all gifts made during the last 10 years must be taken into account (except that no gift made before April 1975, when CTT was introduced, is taxable).

Tax is payable at the rates in force at the date of the gift and, except on death, this 10 year rule is used only for calculating what tax is payable on the gift in question; it does not alter the tax paid, if any, on previous gifts in the donor's lifetime.

To find the rate of tax payable when a person dies, therefore, you have to find out what gifts the deceased made within the previous 10 years because the point on the scale for the rate of tax applicable to the estate at the date of death depends on this.

The position is made more complicated by the fact that lifetime gifts are taxed on a different scale, at lower rates than are payable on someone's death.

However, where gifts have been made within 3 years before the date of death they are taxed at the higher rate, the one applicable to death. So, it is also necessary to know what gifts were made within this period. If tax was paid on such gifts, the extra tax payable at the time of the death will be the difference between the lifetime and the death rate. The rule only operates to increase the rate at which tax is payable where tax was actually paid on a lifetime transfer. Where, on a lifetime gift, there was no tax payable for any reason, there cannot be any further tax payable simply because of the death of the donor within 3 years.

Here is an example to show how the rules work – on the assumption that for the period under consideration the rules and rates remain constant as they exist at present. (It should be borne in mind that tax is payable in accordance with the rates in force at the time of the gift or death.)

Tax is payable in accordance with the table on page 34; column A for lifetime gifts and column B for a person's estate at the date of his death, and also for gifts made within 3 years of the date of the gift.

On 1 January 1983, John, who had not before made any gifts other than 'wholly exempt' ones such as small Christmas or birthday presents, makes a taxable gift of £2,000 to his brother David. There will be no tax payable because the first £55,000 is taxed at nil-rate. The gift has to be set off against part of the nil-rate band, though, because it will affect the tax payable on later gifts.

On 1 January 1985, John gives his house to his daughter Susan. The house is worth £45,000. Tax will be charged on the lifetime scale on the cumulative total of transfers, that is gifts, made within the last 10 years. He still has £35,000 of his nil-rate band left, so £10,000 of the gift to Susan is taxable on the lifetime scale at 15 per cent, and tax of £1500 must be paid (assuming that Susan pays the tax).

On 1 January 1994 John gives a further £20,000 to David. In the last 10 years he has made £45,000 of transfers (because of the gift of his house to Susan). The gift in 1983 has fallen out of account at this point, because more than 10 years have passed since it was made. So he still has got £10,000 taxable at nil-rates and £10,000 taxable at 15 per cent. The tax payable will therefore be £1,500, again.

On 1 January 1996 he dies, leaving a total taxable estate of £175,000. Under his will, he gives it all to his two children Susan and James equally. All of this will be taxable on the death scale, whose rates are always higher than the lifetime rates. To work out at what rate tax is payable, you have to look back ten years and cumulate the gifts made in the last 10 years. The 1983 gift and the 1985 gift have both fallen out of account; the gift in 1994 is within this period. Therefore only £35,000 (i.e. £55,000 less the £20,000 gift in 1994) is taxable at the nil-rate.

Using column B the next £20,000 is taxable at 30 per cent = £6,000
the next £25,000 is taxable at 35 per cent = £8,750
the next £30,000 is taxable at 40 per cent = £12,000
the next £35,000 is taxable at 45 per cent = £15,750
the next £30,000 is taxable at 50 per cent = £15,000

the total tax on £175,000 is £57,500

There is one further point: as a result of the death being within 3 years of the gift of 1 January 1994, that gift will be taxed at the death rates rather than the lifetime rates. At death rates, the tax on £10,000 will be at 30 per cent, and so an extra £1,500 tax must be paid out of the estate as a result of John's death.

	Capital Transfer Tax	
	A	**B**
value of gift	lifetime	death
between	rate of tax	rate of tax
£ £	per cent	per cent
0– 55,000	nil	nil
55,000– 75,000	15	30
75,000– 100,000	17½	35
100,000– 130,000	20	40
130,000– 165,000	22½	45
165,000– 200,000	25	50
200,000– 250,000	30	55
250,000– 650,000	35	60
650,000–1,250,000	40	65
1,250,000–2,500,000	45	70
2,500,000 and above	50	75

'free' gifts

There are a number of exemptions which allow both gifts in lifetime and property on death to be transferred without incurring liability to CTT.

Each year, you are allowed to give £3,000 away with no CTT consequences at all. Furthermore, if any of this exemption is not used in a year (which runs from 6 April to 5 April each year), the unused part can be carried forward for one year, but no more than one year. The current year's exemption has to be used before that brought forward from the previous year.

So, if in year 1 £2,000 is given away, £4,000 could be given away in year 2. But if in year 2 only £2,000 is given away then only £1,000 can be carried forward to year 3. If £3,000 had been given away in year 2 then no carry-forward to year 3 would be allowed. The extra £1,000 available from year 1 becomes worthless.

Also bequests up to £250,000 to charities, and up to £100,000 to political parties are exempt. These amounts can be made up of any number of charitable and political bequests. *From 15 March 1983, all gifts to charities are exempt, without limit.*

stop press

In the budget speech on 15 March 1983, the Chancellor announced that new scales of rates would apply with effect from 6 April 1983. (The 'stop-press' table on page 40 gives the new figures.)

The following example shows how the rules work where the rates change in the ten-year period:

On 1 January 1983 Brian, a widower who has not previously made any gifts other than wholly exempt ones, gives £20,000 to each of his sons, Sam and Stephen, and £17,000 to his sister Sally. Applying the rates for transfers prior to April 1983, £55,000 of the total transfer of £57,000 is taxed at nil rate, £2,000 is taxed at 15 per cent. So, tax of £300 has to be paid, and this is borne by Sam, Stephen and Sally in the proportions of their gift (20:20:17).

On 1 June 1983, Brian gives £10,000 to his mother Mary. Tax is payable by reference to the table correct at that time, that is the one applying to transfers after 5 April 1983. Brian is allowed £60,000 at nil rate; his transfers so far in the last ten years come to £57,000. So £3,000 of his gift to Mary is taxed at nil rate and the balance of £7,000 is taxed at 15 per cent, so that Mary has to pay £1,050.

This does not in any way affect the tax paid on the gift of 1 January, because that was quite correctly paid on the scale in force at that time.

On 1 October 1983 Brian dies, leaving all his property to Sam and Stephen equally. His estate totalled £65,000. Adding together the transfers in the last 10 years, he had made £67,000 of gifts. So of the £65,000 he leaves,

£13,000 is taxed at 30 per cent = £ 3,900
£30,000 is taxed at 35 per cent = £10,500
£22,000 is taxed at 40 per cent = £ 8,800
Total tax   £23,200.

However, Brian had made some gifts within 3 years of the date of his death, and these have to be taxed at death rates, too. Because they are taxed at death rates applicable to the time of death, all of the first gift of £57,000 is now taxed at nil rate, so no further tax is payable on this (again, this does not affect the tax paid on the original gift). Of the gift of 1 June, again £3,000 is within the nil rate band; £7,000 has to be taxed at 30 per cent, so an extra 15 per cent (i.e. £1,050) must be paid.

So the total capital transfer tax paid on Brian's death will be £24,250 (£23,200 plus £1,050 due to the higher death rate tax on part of the gift).

husband and wife

The most important exemption both during lifetime and on death is that all property passing between a husband and a wife is exempt.

Obviously, you must always bear in mind the capital which you and your wife or husband will require for the rest of your lives and for the rest of the survivor's life. But because of the increasing rates at which tax is payable, the higher scale operating for transfers on death, and also the fact that only those transfers made within the last 10 years have to be cumulated, it can effect large savings of tax to give property away sooner rather than later where this can be spared. If possible, it is always better – from the CTT point of view – for property in the estates of husband and wife to pass directly to children rather than passing from, say, the husband to the wife and then all the property passing on her subsequent death to the children.

For example, if John had had an estate of £65,000 on his death and he had made no previous taxable gifts (if he had, for instance made large gifts more than 10 years ago and had since then only been using his annual exemptions) and his estate was to pass to his wife, Jean, then no tax would be payable. Later, however, Jean dies. She also had property of her own, worth £65,000. So her total estate on her death was £130,000.

The total tax payable will be £55,000 at nil.

£20,000 at 30 per cent = £6,000
£25,000 at 35 per cent = £8,750
£30,000 at 40 per cent = £12,000
Total tax payable = £26,750

(This assumes that the rates remained constant, with no changes announced by the Chancellor.)

However, if John's property had passed to Susan and James equally and none of it had gone to Jean, the tax payable would have been £3,000 on John's death (instead of nil) but only a further £3,000 on Jean's death, so achieving a tax saving of £20,750. The only slight disadvantage is that the first £3,000 of tax payable has to be paid on the earlier death, and therefore sooner than would otherwise be the case. But this is outweighed by the greater saving on Jean's death.

The ultimate saving is achieved by making sure that the same top rate of tax is payable on both the husband's and wife's estates. Unless there is new legislation and provided that rates remain constant between the time of the husband's death and the wife's death, this can be done by making lifetime gift and provisions in the will in such a way as to get the size of the two estates to be the same at the date of each death.

In any event, very substantial savings can be achieved provided the nil-rate band is fully used in both estates. It is wasted where less than £55,000 passes to non-exempt beneficiaries.

Anyone who has young children must be careful to ensure the wife has adequate capital to support the children. It would be pointless to make gifts to save tax but leave the wife with insufficient capital. But these savings can often be used when the family is older.

where there are no young children
By leaving up to £55,000 to the children direct (the rest presumably going to the spouse) you save tax in the long run by taking advantage of the exemption available for the first £55,000 of property left to anyone other than the spouse. But what you give to your spouse on your death will be added to his or her estate when he or she dies and may push up the rate of capital transfer tax to be paid.

Quite apart from CTT, a will of a man or woman with grown-up children is anyway likely to look quite different from that of a younger person because there is no need for the elaborate provisions dealing with children under age. Here is an example of a will of a man whose children are grown up. His total property is worth about £120,000, and he has made no previous taxable gifts.

WILL of Peter Thomas Seaton
of The Red House, Pedham Road, Hemblighton, Norfolk, retired builder

1. I revoke all previous wills and codicils
2. I appoint my wife Margery and my daughter Barbara Ann Millington of 84 Sandy Road, Chesterfield, Derbyshire to be my executors. If either of them has died or cannot or will not act, I appoint my friend Jeremy Mitchell of 17 Brundall Road, Saithe, Norfolk to act instead.
3. I give the following legacies:
   (1) to my daughter Barbara the sum of £15,000
   (2) to my daughter Francesca the sum of £12,000
   (3) to my son Matthew the sum of £12,000
   (4) to my friend Jeremy Mitchell the sum of £10,000

4. I give the following bequests:
    (1) to my friend Edward Raleigh of Kingswood, Lymington Drive, Poole, Dorset, my stamp collection
    (2) to my brother Andrew Basil Seaton my car
    (3) to my son Matthew my collection of prints
    (4) to my daughter Barbara my picture 'Morning at Menton' by Leger
    (5) to my daughter Francesca my clocks, watches, trinkets, cuff links and cut glassware.
5. I give the rest of my estate to my wife Margery.
6. If my wife Margery dies before me, I leave my personal effects, furniture and chattels to my daughter Francesca and the rest of my estate shall be divided equally between my three children, Barbara, Francesca and Matthew.
7. I wish to be cremated.

Date: ....
Signature: ....
Signed by Peter Thomas Seaton as his will in the presence of both of us, who then as witnesses have signed below in his presence, and the presence of each other:

....
....

This will is framed with CTT in mind. In particular, it makes use of the available exemption of the first £55,000 of property by providing for legacies of £49,000 in cash, and bequests of individual items amounting to perhaps another £5,000, before providing for the rest to go to the widow.

A reference to codicils in a revocation clause means that the present will is to revoke all previous testamentary provisions – any older will and any formal supplements or alterations to that will, known as codicils. It is a good idea to include codicils in a revocation clause, just in case.

if the house is jointly-owned
Jointly held property may have to be considered in this context. If, for instance, the house is jointly owned by husband and wife, it would be normal to expect that on the death of one of them, the survivor would take the house. In the case of joint tenancy, this would happen automatically. In

the case of a tenancy in common, it could pass under the terms of the will. In either case, no CTT would be payable, because the transfer on death of the dead person's share in the house would be to a surviving spouse. However, in the case of property owned jointly by, say, a mother and daughter, or two friends, liability to CTT would arise on half the value of the house.

Where the house is held on a tenancy in common by husband and wife, it is possible (and useful for CTT purposes) to avoid each half share going to the other spouse by giving it to the children. (If the property is held as joint tenancy, it must first be converted into a tenancy in common; this can be done by simply stating, in writing, 'I wish to sever the joint tenancy with X'). A provision can be included that the property cannot be sold without the consent of the surviving spouse, and so, effectively, that person will be able to live there as long as he or she wants. There could also be a provision that if the house is sold, and another property bought, the same provisions should apply, so that the family could move to a new house if it wished.

If you feel this possibility is something you would like to consider, you should, however, seek professional advice.

some other ways of saving CTT
There are other ways in which CTT may be saved, but these are more elaborate and beyond the scope of this book. Professional advice should be sought; they are mentioned here just so that you can give them consideration.

For instance, it is possible to include a complicated provision in a will where for the period of 2 years from a person's death the estate is held on a trust for a class of people (usually the husband or wife, children, brothers and sisters) and the executors may, at their discretion, pay out the capital to any member of the class at any time within that period. This can therefore be used to obtain efficient CTT treatment of a person's property at death and is very flexible because the decision as to who will get what part of the property can be left for up to 2 years after death. In this way, even though it may not ultimately be the most efficient distribution of property for CTT purposes (which would be leaving it all to the children), the wife could get the capital, or part of it, from the estate if and when she needs it, and the decision to pay it to her can be made at the last moment, thus preserving the possibilities of at least reducing the tax burden.

If you think this provision of establishing what is called a discretionary trust may suit your circumstances, you should get legal advice in drawing up your will.

future CTT rates

One final point to bear in mind is that the bands in columns A and B of the table on page 34 are now index-linked each year in accordance with the rise in the Retail Prices Index in December each year. The new scale applies from each following April. The threshold of each band is increased upwards by the same percentage as the rise in the Retail Prices Index and then rounded up to the nearest £1,000. This provision operates unless parliament decides otherwise. In practice, it is likely that after the budget statement each year a new scale of rates will be published.

In the budget speech on 15 March 1983, the Chancellor announced that the following scales of rates would apply with effect from 6 April 1983.

		A	B
value of gift between		*lifetime rate of tax*	*death rate of tax*
£	*£*	*per cent*	*per cent*
0–	60,000	nil	nil
60,000–	80,000	15	30
80,000–	110,000	17$\frac{1}{2}$	35
110,000–	140,000	20	40
140,000–	175,000	22$\frac{1}{2}$	45
175,000–	220,000	25	50
220,000–	270,000	30	55
270,000–	700,000	35	60
700,000–	1,325,000	40	65
1,325,000–	2,650,000	45	70
2,650,000 and above		50	75

Capital Transfer Tax after 5 April 1983

Some complicated calculations may be required to work out the tax payable either on a lifetime gift or when someone dies, because all transfers within the previous ten years have to be accumulated and this can be confusing where the rates of tax have been altered in that period. But it is really fairly straightforward if you bear in mind always that it is the table of rates correct at the time each gift is made to which reference must be made to find out the tax payable in relation to that gift. (An example is given on page 35.)

signing the will

A will does not have to state the date on which it was signed, but it is much better that it should. The date can appear at the beginning or the end, it does not matter which. Perhaps if it is at the end, just above the place for signing, there is slightly less chance of forgetting to fill in the date when the will is actually signed. Lawyers tend to set out the date in full 'the twenty-seventh day of March one thousand nine hundred and eighty three'. Even 'in the year of Our Lord . . .' is not completely extinct today. There is nothing wrong with putting '27 March 1983', provided it is written legibly in the space on the will meant for it. The date may be put in before the will is finally signed in the presence of the witnesses.

witnesses to the signature

Anyone who is left anything in the will should not be a witness, and neither should the wife or husband of anyone who is left anything in it. Where this happens, the will is legally valid – in other words, these witnesses are perfectly all right as witnesses – but they lose their legacies; the will is interpreted as if the gift to the witness, or the spouse of the witness, were cut out of it. Secondly, a blind person should not be a witness. Also, it is probably best to avoid having someone under age to be a witness, although there is nothing in law about it.

The will must be signed by the testator, the person whose will it is, within the sight of two witnesses, who should both be present together when he actually signs.

It will be invalid unless both the witnesses are physically present when the will is signed, although, strictly speaking, it is still a valid will if the testator acknowledges his previously written signature – as distinct from signing there and then – in the joint presence of the two witnesses. It is best that they should both actually watch as the signature goes on, although it is sufficient if they are standing or sitting in such a position that they could have seen the signing, if they had looked in the right direction. The testator must sign first, and the witnesses afterwards; the other way around will not do. Each witness must sign in the presence of the testator, but one witness does not have to be present when the other witness is signing. If Matthew Seaton were to sign his will in the presence of Robert Jones and Michael Smith, and then, before either of them began to sign, Matthew went out of the room, and while he was out of the room, Robert and Michael signed as witnesses, the will would be invalid. The same would apply if only one of the witnesses signed out of the presence of the testator, but it would be valid if Matthew remained after signing in the presence of both the witnesses, and Robert left the room while Michael signed and then Matthew was still present when Robert returns.

To sum up, then: the person making the will must be there all the time that anybody is signing; both the witnesses must be there when the testator signs; it is not necessary for each witness to be present when the other witness signs. To be on the safe side, however, the best thing is to make sure that all three of them are present throughout all the signing by all three of them.

attestation clause

The will should contain an attestation clause, that is, a clause explaining the process of signing and witnessing. If the clause were missing, then, after the testator's death, when it comes to proving the will, it would be necessary to have an affidavit – a sworn statement – from one of the witnesses to explain what happened when the will was signed and witnessed. This could cause great difficulties if the witnesses could not be traced, or were dead. So a properly worded attestation clause, though not strictly necessary, should be included in a will.

Lawyers tend to favour rather a long attestation clause. One may find something like this: 'Signed by the said Matthew John Seaton as and for his last will and testament in the presence of us both present at the same time, who at his request, in his presence and in the presence of each other have hereunto subscribed our names as witnesses.' But it is enough just to say: 'Signed by Matthew John Seaton in our presence, and then by us in his'.

It is also not strictly necessary for the witnesses to write their addresses on the will. Their signature is all that is legally required. But, once again, it is much better if they do add their address, and perhaps their occupation as well, so that if there were any question raised later about what happened at the time, they can more easily be traced. For the same reason, if either of their signatures is such as to make the surname illegible, it is not a bad idea to write the name in block letters underneath the signature.

when the will is long

If your will runs to more than one page, it is a good idea to sign each page at the bottom, and to ask the two witnesses to do the same, immediately after the last line of writing, without leaving any gap. This is not a legal requirement, but it does help to prevent any forgery of your will, in the form of adding a clause to the bottom of a page, or even an extra page. If, after your death, a clause saying 'I give £5,000 to William Sykes' appeared at the foot of a page, you would not be there to explain that it was not there when you signed the will. Signing each page is more important still when the will extends to more than one sheet of paper. It is better not to leave blank the back page of any sheet of paper on which your will is written. Either continue with the clauses on to the back of each page, or draw a line right across the blank space, and put your initials at the top and bottom of the line. Ask the witnesses to do the same. It should be your aim to make any tampering with your will as difficult as possible, and at the same time make it obvious which are the sheets of paper which comprise your will, each sheet of which should bear your signature at the bottom. Make sure that each page of your will is numbered, so that no one can craftily slip in a couple of extra pages containing benefits to himself. Finally, do not pin anything to your will and make sure that no pin holes appear in it. Such holes may give the impression that a sheet of paper forming part of your will was at one time attached to it, but has now disappeared.

In Matthew's will, therefore, he and the two witnesses as well as signing the full attestation at the end of the will, should each sign at the bottom of the first page. If below the witnesses' signatures on the back of the sheet there is more than the usual bottom-of-a-page space, it is also sensible to 'line-off' the space, and for Matthew and the witnesses to sign each end of the line.

When the process of signing and witnessing is over, how then does the will appear? Take the examples already considered. Picking up Matthew Seaton's will at the last part of the last clause as it was prepared, it will now continue through to the end to look like this:

. . . if that parent had lived long enough.

Date: 5 April 1983.
Signature: M. J. Seaton.
Signed by Matthew John Seaton in our presence and then by us in his:
Margery Abrahams   M. B. Roberts
22 Twintree Avenue   'The Reddings', Park Avenue
Minford, Surrey   Little Minford, Surrey
Sales Manager   Schoolmaster.

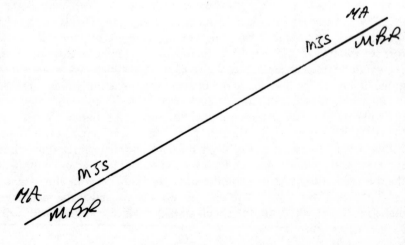

what to do with the will

From the moment the will is signed and witnessed it is valid. Matthew Seaton may safely die at any time, secure in the knowledge that his testamentary wishes have been legally expressed.

There is no law in England and Wales requiring that wills must be registered before death. It is up to the testator himself to find a safe place for his will, to put it there, and to let his relatives know where it is. Quite a few people lodge their will in their bank. If you have a safe at home, this is an obvious place in which to put your will. Failing that, perhaps the best place for your will is wherever you keep your other important documents: marriage and birth certificates, savings certificates, title deeds of the house, and so on. Put the will in an envelope, sealing it if you want to, and write on the outside your full name, the word WILL in large letters and the date. There is no stamp duty on a will, so no further formalities are required before putting the will away safely.

Apart from telling your immediate relatives where your will is, you should also tell your executors where it is. Tell them when the will has been made, and confirm that the will appoints them as executors. If the will is lodged at the bank, it may be helpful to make the executor known to the bank, perhaps even introduce him or her personally to the manager, so that there will be no difficulty or delay about handing over the will to the executor. If the will is locked away in your house or your office, tell the executors where the key is. Whether or not you tell your executors (or your relatives) who is going to inherit your property under your will is entirely up to you; there is no legal requirement. But you should keep your executors informed about what you possess. A list, setting out in round figures what you own, could well be placed with your will for safe custody, and from time to time you should revise the list to keep it up to date.

You should, perhaps, have told your executors, when asking whether they were willing to accept the appointment, what your property consisted of and its approximate value, so that they knew in advance what was the measure of the job they were being asked to take on. As time goes by, and your situation develops and changes, they should be kept informed on how your current wealth stands, especially if you acquire unusual assets. Your object should be to make things as easy as possible for them when you die. Any tendency to be secretive about your assets is likely to make life more difficult for your executors.

You should also keep them up to date on where the essential documents are to be found. The logical course, obviously, is to keep things like share certificates, building society share accounts, savings books, savings certificates, insurance policies, title deeds and all similar documents in one place, a family safe, for instance, or a locked drawer, maybe. This is probably the same place as where your will itself is kept. If you keep your affairs tidy and orderly so far as possible, when the time comes for your executors to act, they will not find that they have taken on an investigation, instead of an administration.

depositing a will
If you want to, you can deposit your will at Somerset House, strictly speaking the Principal Registry, Family Division, Somerset House, Strand, London WC2R 1LP. The will has to be in a sealed envelope, on which there is an endorsement giving the names and addresses of the executors who must have been informed that the will has been lodged. The date of the will, your date of birth and full name and address have to be on the envelope, too, and your signature must be witnessed on it. You can post or take the envelope in person, either to Somerset House or to any district probate registry or sub-registry. The fee is £1. You will be given a deposit certificate which has to be produced if the will is to be withdrawn. The advantage of this system is that the existence and whereabouts of the will is known to the executors; the disadvantage is that you have to make a written request to the principal registry to bave the will returned if you want to make any alteration.

alterations

Any obvious alterations made on the face of a will are presumed – until the contrary is proved – to have been made after the original signing and witnessing took place, and so not to form part of the legally valid will. Furthermore, any legacy which appears underneath your signature is not valid.

You may want to alter your will, owing to a change in circumstances, such as a death, or a change of heart following a difference of opinion, for instance. You must not cross bits out of your will, or write bits in, or make any alterations whatsoever on it. The will is valid in the form in which it stood on the day it was signed. Theoretically, you could make subsequent alterations on the will itself by signing the altered will and having that new signature witnessed again, as was done when the will was first signed. But this is messy and unsatisfactory, and quite the wrong way to go about making alterations to a will.

codicils

If all you want to do is to make a simple alteration to your will as it stands, you could do this by making a codicil. This really is nothing more than a supplement to a will, which makes some alteration to it but leaves the rest of it standing. For instance, you may wish to increase a cash legacy, to take account of inflation since you made the will.

To find out the whole of the testator's wishes, both the will and the codicil have to be considered. A codicil, to be valid, must be signed and witnessed in exactly the same way as a will. It has to be signed by the testator in the presence of two witnesses and they must both sign it in the presence of the testator. These witnesses do not have to be the same two who witnessed the original will. Here is an example:

This is the first codicil to the will, dated 5 April 1983, of me Matthew John Seaton of 14 Twintree Avenue, Minford, Surrey.

1. I revoke the bequest of my golf clubs, bag and trolley to my nephew Donald Millington.
2. I give £250 to my brother Robert Seaton.
3. In all other respects, I confirm my will.

Date: 5 October 1983.
Signature: M. J. Seaton.

Signed by Matthew John Seaton in our presence and then by us in his:

Ivy Gurney	Andrew Roth
'The Larches'	140 Latchmoor Grove
Greta Grove	Gerrards Cross, Bucks.
Eastbourne.	Journalist.
Bookseller.	

Some people make quite a few codicils. There is no limit on how many you may make. But a codicil is only suitable for a straightforward alteration to a will. For anything more than that, it is better to make a completely new will. If the will was quite short in the first place, it is probably better to make a completely new will anyway, and not bother with making a codicil.

revocation

If you make a later will, it should, of course, contain the clause which revokes the previous will. Once the later will is signed, and so in force, it is best to destroy the previous one, just in case, years later when you die, the old will is found among your papers, and mistaken for the one you meant to apply.

– by destruction

There are two other ways of revoking a will besides a specific clause in a later will mentioning revocation. The first is where, with the intention of revoking it, you burn it, tear it up, or in some other way destroy it. The emphasis here is on the words 'with the intention of revoking it'. If your will were to be accidentally burnt, whether by you or by someone else, it would not be revoked by that. There have, in fact, been cases where a will has been declared valid after the testator's death, the original having been accidentally destroyed. In one case, for instance, the torn-up pieces were reassembled and proved as a valid will, where it was shown that it was torn up in mistake for an old letter.

The testator himself must burn the will, or tear it up, in order for it to be effectively revoked. Alternatively, it may be done by someone at his direction and in his presence. But your will would not be revoked, for example, if you were to write to the bank manager who kept it, telling him to destroy it, even if he did so. The destruction has to take place in your presence and if this does not happen the will is not revoked until, of course, a subsequent will is made which contains a revocation clause.

– by marriage

The other way of revoking a will is the most surprising and the one that is most easily forgotten: getting married. The law supposes that a man or a woman who has made a will and later gets married, automatically wishes that the will should no longer stand. As a result, merely to get married, without saying anything about an existing will, revokes the will. This can have some curious results. Imagine that a widow with young children has made a will leaving her property to the children. Some years later she marries again. She must make a new will after the second marriage, otherwise her husband would inherit all the property up to £40,000, her children getting nothing, as she would have died intestate, her will having been revoked by her second marriage.

– not always revoked by marriage

It is, however, possible to make a will which says that it is made in contemplation of a forthcoming marriage.

The will must state that it is made in contemplation of marriage to a particular person, who must be named, and it must also state that the testator intends that the will shall not be revoked by his marriage to that person. Such a will is not revoked by that marriage but, should that marriage never happen and, instead, the testator marries someone else, the will is then revoked. If no marriage whatever takes place, the will, of course, will remain effective.

the effect of divorce

Divorce, on the other hand, does not automatically revoke all the provisions of a will. The effect of a divorce is that any appointment of the former spouse as an executor will be of no effect, and any gift in the will to the former spouse will be treated as if the former spouse had died before the testator. Where the gift is a specific one, for example of a house or '£10,000', such property will go to whoever is entitled to the residue of the estate. But where, under the term of the will, the former spouse is given the rest of the estate, it will be dealt with in accordance with the intestacy rules. If Matthew and Emma, in the earlier example of Matthew's will, had divorced and no alterations were made to the wills, then the executors would have been David Seaton and Andrew Shervington. Clause 7 would have been of no effect and clause 8 would have taken effect as if Emma had died before Matthew. The rest of the will, including the legacies in clauses 5 and 6, would remain unaffected.

later

Once you have made a will, it is easy to tuck it away safely and forget about it for ever. But you should review your will now and again; every couple of years is not too frequent. You may find that nothing needs changing. On the other hand, there could be quite substantial changes that need to be made. If so, you will have to start the whole process over again.

probate

The people who deal with what you own when you die are called your personal representatives. If they are appointed by a valid will, they are known as executors; when they were not appointed in this way, as happens on an intestacy, the personal representatives are known as administrators.

In either case, they usually have to obtain an official document from the High Court to show that they are the ones with legal authority to deal with the property. In the case of executors, who are said to prove the will, this document is called a grant of probate, also referred to as a probate of the will, or, for short, the probate. Administrators, on the other hand, obtain a grant of letters of administration. The document which constitutes the probate or the letters of administration is sometimes referred to as the grant. The task of executors as well as of administrators is referred to as the administration of the estate.

when no grant is needed
It is not always essential to take out a grant of probate or letters of administration. If the property left behind consists only of cash (that is, bank notes and coins) and personal effects such as furniture and a car (and not, for instance, any shares, bank accounts, pension arrears or house), no formal steps to prove the right of the relatives to their inheritance need be taken. They can immediately take physical possession of everything. But the will should never be destroyed. Of course, if there is a dispute amongst them as to who shall have what, or how it is to be organised, it may be necessary to put the whole matter on a proper legal footing by taking out a grant.

There are some other kinds of property which can be handed over without much formality. Where, for instance, the deceased held not more than £1,500 in national savings with the Department for National Savings, that amount (together with the interest to the date of payment) can be paid to the person now entitled to it, without a grant being taken out at all. The same applies to money held in savings banks, friendly societies and certain pension funds. The sum involved in the savings bank (or similar) must not exceed £1,500, but the total value of the estate (including the money in the savings bank) may be more than £1,500. The procedure for obtaining the money is usually simple. The relative or other person who is entitled to claim the money writes to the savings bank or other organisation concerned, explaining the circumstances, and asking to be sent the appropriate form. This must then be completed and returned with a £1.50 death certificate ('certificate for certain statutory purposes') and, where appropriate, the marriage certificate. (However, the savings bank or other body can, at its discretion, require you to take out a grant even if the amount involved is under £1,500.)

There was a system of nominating some kinds of property in favour of a particular person, to take effect on death, for example the money in a National Savings Bank account, and national savings certificates, also British Savings Bonds and certain specified government stock. In 1981, nominations facilities were withdrawn and no new nominations can now be made. But such nominations as have been made will be honoured and dealt with as before.

The person to whom savings are nominated can apply to have them in cash or transferred into his name, on producing the death certificate and without producing a grant of probate of letters of administration. Nomination is quite distinct from the procedure for obtaining payment in cases under £1,500, and applies irrespective of the amount involved, provided that there has been a nomination. If the value of the property nominated exceeds £3,000, the savings bank may require a certificate from the Inland Revenue to show that the CTT has been taken care of. (Nomination is not a way of escaping CTT: the amount that has been nominated has to be accounted for as part of the estate.)

A nomination made in this way applies whether or not a will mentions it and is not revoked or affected by a will made afterwards. A nomination is revoked by signing the special form, or by the death of the person in whose favour the nomination was made before the death of the person who made it (but not by the marriage of the nominator, because nomination bypasses the will).

what is involved

In most cases, an administration by personal representatives follows roughly this pattern:

Find out the nature and value of the assets in the estate.

Find out details of the debts (advertise for creditors, if relevant).

Prepare a detailed list of the estate and of the debts, for the purpose of CTT.

Work out roughly the amount of CTT and arrange any necessary overdraft or other credit.

Prepare and send off the documents required by the Inland Revenue and probate registry.

Visit the probate registry in person to swear the papers.

Pay the CTT.

Receive the grant of probate or letters of administration.

Send an official copy of the grant to the bank, the insurance company, and so on, and get from them what belongs to the estate.

Sell any property.

Pay the debts.

Pay the legacies; hand over the bequests.

Distribute or invest the residue.

when to consult a solicitor

Any one of a number of complexities can arise in connection with winding up an estate. Often the personal representatives are busy people, without the time to cope with the legal side of an administration and would not contemplate administering an estate without employing a solicitor. In many cases, a solicitor's services are essential: when the deceased owned his own business, for instance, or was a partner in a firm, or was involved in an insurance syndicate, or where there is agricultural property, or when family trusts are involved (stemming from the deceased's parents, perhaps, or from a marriage settlement).

If the deceased left no will and the estate comes to more than £40,000 (after deducting the value of the personal effects including the car) the spouse will get a life interest, provided that there are children as well, of whatever age. In this case, the complications likely to arise from the life interest make a solicitor's advice and help almost essential. The same applies where, on an intestacy or under the will, some of the property is to pass to children who are at present under age. Their rights are called minority interests, and particular legal problems can arise regarding them. This is so whether the children are 17 weeks, 17 months or 17 years old.

Another situation which usually demands consulting a solicitor is where, on an intestacy, some long forgotten relative is entitled to a share in the estate. For example, a brother – perhaps the black sheep of the family – may have gone to Australia 40 years ago and not been heard of since. In such a case, the australian brother is entitled, if the decreased left no will, to the same share as the sister who lovingly nursed the deceased through his last years of illness. The problems involved in tracing relatives who have apparently disappeared generally require expert handling, as does the situation if they are not in fact found.

Home-made wills, particularly on some of the printed forms, sometimes contain ambiguities or irregularities which can create difficulties and legal help about the interpretation may be needed at some stage.

If the estate is insolvent – if the debts exceed the value of the assets – a solicitor needs to be consulted. The same applies where, although the estate is solvent, there is not sufficient to pay all the legacies in full or there is no residue.

A solicitor's fees for dealing with an estate are paid out of the deceased's property. They are a proper expense, like the funeral expenses, and the CTT; the personal representatives do not have to pay them out of their own pockets. But they have to be paid nevertheless, and it is normally the residuary legatee who bears them. He is the person who, under the will, is to receive the rest of the deceased's property after paying out everything else, including these expenses.

The amount charged by solicitors for work of this kind depends on a number of factors, including the amount of work involved, the urgency of the case and the value of the estate. There are not many estates where the solicitor's fees will be less than £100, and in a large number of cases they will be much more. There is no longer a recommended scale fee. The Law Society used to suggest, as a guide, the following as a basis for fees in normal probate cases: on a gross estate between £2,000 and £10,000, a rate of 3 per cent of the gross estate; on the next £40,000 (that is, between £10,000 and £50,000), 2½ per cent of the gross estate; lower rates applied above that. Lately, there is a suggestion that the fee should be based on one per cent of the gross estate.

The Law Society's suggested percentage is no more than a guide, and not necessarily strictly adhered to. In addition, there are probate registry fees, fees for oaths, and other out of pocket expenses to be paid, not to mention the CTT. These expenses have to be paid, whether a solicitor is instructed or not. But the fees paid to the solicitor can be saved if the personal representatives deal with the administration of the estate themselves.

do-it-yourself

There are precedents for people going about some enterprise which is generally the province of the legal profession, and without in fact having any assistance from that direction. Some litigants in person, as they are called, have taken cases to court alone. Many laymen have bought a house without a solicitor.

Whereas the litigant in person and the do-it-yourself house buyer must feel his way uncertainly through the devious ways lawyers have made for themselves, the personal representative will find that there is a special machinery set up just for him. There is a personal application department in each of the probate registries, which has special staff, special forms and special procedures designed to smooth the path of the inexperienced layman.

But the help and advice given by the personal application department of a probate registry is confined to getting the grant of probate or letters of administration, and the personal representative is generally left to find out for himself – by reading this book, for instance – what goes before and what come after.

the administration of an estate

Mary Blake has died. Robert, her son, and Matthew Seaton, her son-in-law, are her executors. Matthew and Robert have agreed that they will not instruct a solicitor in connection with the administration of the estate. This is the story of what they did.

Matthew is the businesslike member of the family, and it was natural that he took charge of events. Matthew had known of his appointment as one of the executors, but had never been shown the will itself. The will had been drawn up by a solicitor and put in the Blakes' deed box. If the will is lodged in the bank, the executor has to sign for it if he collects it in person; or acknowledge its safe receipt in writing if it is sent to him by post. Where several executors are named in the will, the bank may ask for all their signatures but should release the will to one of them on the understanding that in due course all the executors will sign an acknowledgement.

Matthew read the will at once to see what is said about burial or cremation. He had no intention of arranging a formal reading of the will to the family after the funeral. This ritual happens mostly in the world of fiction.

Mary Blake's will

THIS IS THE LAST WILL AND TESTAMENT of me MARY JOSEPHINE BLAKE of The Firs, Willow Lane, Minford, Surrey, widow.

I hereby revoke all former wills and codicils at any time heretofore made by me and declare this to be my last will and testament.

1. I hereby appoint my son Robert Anthony Blake of Wringapeak Farm, Woody Bay, North Devon and my son-in-law Matthew John Seaton of 14 Twintree Avenue, Minford, in the county of Surrey, to be the executors and trustees of this my will.
2. I bequeath my diamond and garnet brooch to my niece Barbara S. Forbes and the rest of my jewellery to my daughter Emma Seaton.
3. I bequeath my carriage clock to my friend Josef Samson.
4. I give the sum of £50 to each of my grandchildren who shall be living at my death.
5. I give the sum of £100 to Mrs Alison Ward of Rose Cottage, Little Minford.

6. I give the sum of £200 to Help the Aged and declare that the receipt of their treasurer for the time being shall be a complete discharge for my executors.
7. I devise my freehold house The Firs, Willow Lane, Minford, Surrey to my son Mark Daniel Blake free of all taxes or duties payable on my death and free of any liability for any outstanding mortgage on the property, together with my furniture and effects therein at the date of my death, and my car.
8. Subject to the payment of my just debts (including any mortgage on my house outstanding at the date of my death) I give devise and bequeath all the rest residue and remainder of my estate both real and personal whatsoever and wheresoever situate unto my trustees UPON TRUST to sell the same (but with the power in their absolute discretion to postpone such sale) and to hold the net proceeds of the sale together with the net rents and profits to arise therefrom until sale UPON TRUST for my children Emma Seaton and Robert Anthony Blake in equal shares.
9. (i) My trustees may invest or apply my residuary estate in any type of property as if they were the absolute beneficial owners.
    (ii) My trustees may apply the actual assets rather than cash if they think fit without requiring the consent of any other person.
10. I express the wish that my body shall be cremated and that my ashes shall be scattered.

IN WITNESS whereof I have hereunto set my hand this sixteenth day of August one thousand nine hundred and seventy two.

Mary J. Blake

Signed by the above named Testatrix Mary Josephine Blake as and for her last Will and Testament in the presence of us both present at the same time together who then at her request in her presence and in the presence of each other hereunto subscribed our names as witness.

Edith Gray   David Tench
14 Bridston Place WC2   her clerk
Solicitor

Matthew read the will at once to see what is said about burial or cremation. He had no intention of arranging a formal reading of the will to the family after the funeral. This ritual happens mostly in the world of fiction.

Mary Blake had been a widow; her will gave the main part of her estate to her 3 children, Emma, Robert and Mark. The first £55,000 of her estate would be immune from CTT, but the whole of the rest of the estate would be liable for tax.

She gave the house to Mark, who was unmarried and lived at home with her at the time of her death. This was sensible. The effect of the will was that any CTT due on the house, and the outstanding mortgage debt, were to be paid out of the estate – the residue of the estate, that is – so that Mark would inherit the house complete, without having to find any money to meet these liabilities. Had it not been for the specific direction in the will to this effect, he would have had to take the house subject to the mortgage on it, and possibly also subject to the proportion of the CTT attributable to the house. That is, he would have had to pay the tax out of his own pocket, and the outstanding mortgage debt, too. This is a rule of interpretation which, so far as CTT is concerned, used to be thought to apply to freehold houses and other freehold land and buildings (following a recent House of Lords decision, it is now no longer certain that the rule applies, and so to avoid doubt a will should state specifically if a beneficiary should take free of CTT).

For leaseholds and personal property (shares, insurance policies, money, bank accounts), the general rule is that the tax is borne by the residue, but that any charge on assets still binds the person who inherits them. For instance, if an overdraft had been secured by the deposit of shares with the bank, the person inheriting the shares, not the residuary legatee, has to settle the overdraft, unless the will says otherwise.

first formalities
The first formality to be arranged was the registration of the death of Mrs Blake with the registrar of births and deaths. The death being registered, Matthew was able to obtain copies of the various death certificates that would be needed on several occasions in the next few weeks.

In Mrs Blake's deed box Matthew found a number of other documents, including a life insurance policy, some national savings certificates, a National Savings Bank book, some premium bonds and some share certificates. Matthew put them back into the box, together with the will, and took the box home.

From the contents of the will, Matthew had satisfied himself that he had full authority to act as an executor with his brother-in-law. A valid will operates from the moment its maker dies, so that an executor has full authority from the moment of a person's death. That authority is effective, even though the will has not yet been formally proved in the way the law demands. When eventually the will is proved, by the issue to the executors of a grant of probate, it merely confirms and makes official the powers they have had since death.

This is an important distinction between probate and letters of administration; administrators have no legal authority to act until the grant of letters of administration is issued to them.

Matthew's brother-in-law, his co-executor who lives in Devon, asked him to deal with the business side of the executorship, and left all the formalities to him. But Matthew made a point of specifically getting his brother-in-law to confirm in writing that this was so. Apart from the courtesy of doing so, this was legally the correct thing to do. Robert was as much an executor as he was, and the proper procedure was for both of them to authorise him to make the necessary arrangements on behalf of both of them.

executor not wishing to act
It is possible for either executor to renounce his right to take out a grant of probate, reserving the right to apply later if the need should arise (for instance if the other executor died, or became mentally incapacitated, before the administration was complete). There may be a number of reasons why someone might wish to renounce the right to probate: for instance, a professional adviser who had not acted for the testator for a number of years, or a relative or friend who had had no contact with the testator for a long period, or simply someone who does not want to be troubled with the chore of the administration. A form of renunciation can be obtained from Oyez Stationery, who have various shops or sales offices throughout the country (the London telephone number is 01-407 8055). Alternatively, at a later stage of the administration, the probate office will send the appropriate piece of paper, called a power reserved letter, for the renouncing executor to sign.

If one of the executors renounces, the substitute automatically comes in (or has also to renounce). In the case of Matthew's own will, if David Seaton had renounced, Andrew Shervington would automatically become an executor (unless he renounced), as if he had been appointed a first-line executor.

It is possible for a person named as executor in the will to appoint an attorney for the purpose of obtaining the grant; the attorney then acts as if he had actually been named as the executor in the will. (The appropriate form for this can be obtained from the Oyez shops.)

It is also possible for a personal representative who has obtained a grant to appoint an attorney to act for him in the rest of the administration. Usually the power lasts for one year and relieves a personal representative of the form-signing part of the administration. It is often useful where the executor is abroad.

However, Matthew and Robert each knew quite a lot about Mary Blake's affairs and both were interested in dealing with the administration, so there was no doubt in their minds that they should proceed, as quickly as possible, to obtain the grant and act in the administration themselves.

Mary Blake's estate

Within a few days, Matthew had assembled most of the available documents regarding the late Mary Blake's property. He started to prepare a list of all the items, with an estimate of the value of each. He was able, from the documents he had found in the house, together with information from his relatives, to compile a provisional list of the assets which made up the estate, estimating high rather than low where he was doubtful.

Provisional details of Mary Blake's estate

		approximately £
National Savings Bank account (plus interest to date of death £8.00)		400
premium bonds		1,500
various stocks and shares (to be valued, but say approximately)		30,000
house: The Firs, Willow Lane, Minford	45,000	
less outstanding mortgage	1,200	
		43,800
3 paintings by well known artists		1,500
other contents (including furniture)		1,000
car		1,350
wedding ring and other jewellery		150
bank account: Barminster Bank (about)		200
insurance policy (plus profits)		3,500
balance of pensions to date of death		50
Other odds and ends, say		300
approximate gross estate		84,450
Debts		
funeral	400	
miscellaneous	100	
		500
approximate net estate		£83,950
CTT (approx)		9,000
		74,950
probate fees and other expenses		200
approximate value to divide according to will		*£74,750*

valuation of assets

Matthew now had a good idea of what was likely to be involved in administering the estate. He prepared a letter to write to the Department for National Savings, the bank manager, and the insurance company, to find out the precise value of some of the assets:

Dear Sir,

Re: Mary Josephine Blake deceased

I am an executor of the will of the late Mary Josephine Blake, who died on 5 January 1983; my co-executor is her son, Robert Anthony Blake of Wringapeak Farm, Woody Bay, North Devon.

The estate includes the asset described below. Please let me know the value of this asset at the date of death.

When the grant of probate has been obtained, I shall send an official copy of it to you for your inspection. Please let me know what formalities (if any) will be involved in obtaining payment of what is due to the estate.

Particulars of asset:
Name in which held:
Description of asset:
Reference number:
Estimated amount of value: £
Additional information:

Yours faithfully,

various national savings

In the letter he sent to the Director, National Savings Bank, Glasgow G58 1SB, he completed the particulars to read as follows:

Particulars of asset:
Name in which held: Mary Josephine Blake
Description of asset: National Savings Bank account
Reference number: George Street, Croydon, No. 5442
Estimated amount or value: £409.25.
Additional information: none

The letter regarding the national savings certificates he sent to the Director, Savings Certificate and SAYE Office, Millburngate House, Durham DH99 1NS, and in this case the completed table said:

Particulars of asset:
Name in which held: Mary J. Blake (or Downie)

Description of asset: savings certificates as listed on attached schedule
Reference number: BPJ9925
Estimated amount or value: £1,000
Additional information: deceased's maiden name was Mary Josephine
Downie; copy of marriage certificate enclosed.

There were quite a number of national savings certificate books, some even going back to before the war, containing certificates from several of the various issues of savings certificates that have been made over the years. Matthew prepared a list on a separate sheet of paper, setting out the savings certificates individually, specifying the cost of each certificate, the number of units represented by it, the serial number on the certificate, and the date of its issue, found by reference to the circular date stamp on it.

The premium savings bonds did not need to have an official valuation. They retain their face value and no question of interest arises. They cannot be nominated or transferred to beneficiaries, but may be left in the ERNIE draws for twelve calendar months following the death, and then cashed. The Bonds and Stock Office, Lytham St Annes, Lancashire FY0 1YN, should be notified of the bond holder's death as soon as possible. Where the value of premium bonds is £1,500 or less, the Bonds and Stock Office may pay out without any grant having been obtained. But where the estate will have to bear some CTT, the Bonds and Stock Office usually refuses to pay out without sight of a grant. For these purposes, any prize a bond may have won since the date of death has to be included in the £1,500 figure.

bank accounts

Mary Blake did not have a Girobank account. When a Girobank account holder dies, his account is administered according to the rules of ordinary banking practice.

Matthew knew that his mother-in-law had kept an account at the Minford branch of the Barminster Bank. He found the cheque book, the paying-in book and the bank statements in a drawer in the house. He wrote the letter to the local manager of the branch, with these details:

Particulars of asset:
Name in which held: Mary J. Blake
Description of asset: current account
Reference number: 00860727
Estimated amount or value: unknown

Additional information required: please let me know
1. whether Mrs Blake kept a deposit account at your branch
2. whether she kept a deed box at your branch, or otherwise deposited any documents or other property with you.

– joint bank account

When assets are held in joint names, it is necessary to fix a value on the share that belonged to the joint owner who died. In the case of a joint bank account, for instance, the executors have to find out the source of the money paid to the credit of the account, as this indicates the proportions in which the credit balance on the date of death was held. If the sole origin of money paid into an account was, for instance, the husband's earnings, it would follow that the whole of the balance in a joint account with his wife was his, and none hers. If she had died first, nothing need have been included in the valuation of her estate, even though she had power to draw on the account during her life. Where both joint holders contributed from their own money to the joint account, it is necessary to identify payments into the account over a period of years, and to calculate the respective total contributions to the account. The credit balance at the date of death would then be divided between the joint account holders in those proportions. If it is impossible to show who contributed what, or if the items in the account are too numerous or complicated to make it possible to distinguish the sources, the balance is considered to be equally held by its joint holders.

This information is needed merely in order to establish how much of the money in the bank has to be included in the CTT returns, not in order to decide how much the survivor can draw from the account.

A joint account has the advantage that the survivor can continue to draw on the account, even though the other account holder has died. As it can take weeks, even months, to get a grant of probate, this allows the survivor to have continued access to ready cash. The balance to the credit of a joint account passes automatically to the survivor and so bypasses the will, unless some specific other agreement was made between the joint account holders.

With any assets held jointly – building society accounts, savings bank accounts, and investments, for instance – a similar calculation must be made.

life insurance

Matthew also wrote a letter of enquiry to the Bridstow Insurance Company. He had found a life assurance policy with that company among the documents in the deed box. It provided for the payment of £3,000 on Mary Blake's death. Matthew found that it was a 'with profits' policy, which meant that in addition to the £3,000 to be paid to the executors by the insurance company, a further amount would be paid. In the letter to the local branch manager of the insurance company, Matthew gave the following particulars:

Particulars of asset:
Name in which held: Mary Josephine Blake
Description of asset: whole life insurance, issued 14 June 1948
Reference number, policy HPX 9421/37
Estimated amount or value: £3,000
Additional information required: as this policy was 'with profits', please let me know the amount of profits that is payable.

Matthew had now set in train the procedure for valuing the property left by his mother-in-law. Even where he knew, or had a fair idea of, the value of an asset, he still wrote to the organisation concerned for a written valuation, in case he should need evidence of the value of any item.

the house

Matthew now turned his attention to the question of valuing the house. Most people have some idea of the current value of the houses in their locality. It is not essential to obtain a professional valuation from a firm of surveyors and valuers. Whether you have a professional valuation or not, your figure will be checked sooner or later by an official called the district valuer. He is employed by the Inland Revenue, but his job has little to do with taxes as such. He is concerned with the valuation of land, houses, factories, shops, offices and so on, for many official purposes, including deciding rateable values. He is an expert on valuation, so there is no point in trying to understate the value of a house. However, for possible saving on CTT, you may as well put down your lowest estimate of value. A point which can be made is that the value is lower because for CTT purposes one has to take the value on a particular day, so it is as if one had to effect a forced sale on that day. The district valuer will query your figure later on if it is too low, but perhaps not if it is on the high side.

However, there may be cases where a higher value should be aimed at, if there is a danger that any future sale may be subject to capital gains tax. The value for CTT is the beneficiary's base cost for CGT purposes, so, a low CTT value may mean a larger gain on any future sale. (Usually the private residence CGT exemption will apply, but this is not invariably the case.)

Matthew estimated the value of The Firs at £45,000. It is possible, where a house is not going to be sold, and where the total estate will be more than £25,000, to agree a value for the house with the district valuer before applying for probate.

if the house was joint property

Whenever a house is held in the joint names of a husband and wife (or any two people), when one of them dies, the value of his or her share has to be decided for CTT purposes. There are two different ways in which property may be held jointly: as joint tenants or as tenants in common. Where a house is owned by joint tenants, the share of the first to die passes to the survivor automatically on death. The survivor of joint tenants acquires the other half-share, in fact, merely by surviving, irrespective of anything the will may say. The terms of the deceased's will do not apply to it at all. In the case of tenants in common, however, the share of the first to die forms part of the estate; that share may, of course, pass to the spouse (or other co-owner) under the will, but that is not the same thing as passing to him or her automatically, as happens when it is a joint tenancy.

It can make a difference to the value of a share in a jointly held house whether it was held as joint tenants or as tenants in common. That would be the first thing for the executor to find out (from the deeds and documents) in the process of valuing the share in a house, on the death of one of the joint owners. If it was held as tenants in common, the executor will have to know the proportions in which it was held in order to estimate the value of the share of the deceased at the date of death. Although it is often held in equal shares, this is not always so.

The vacant possession value at the date of death is the starting point in calculating the value of the deceased's share of the house for CTT. Suppose it is the figure of £38,500. In the case of a joint tenancy or a tenancy in common held in equal shares, that figure must be divided in two, to allow for the share of only the one who died; this would give a figure of £19,250.

But one has not yet arrived at the true net value of the deceased's share. Because it was only a share in a house, and because the other joint owner still has the right to live there, it follows that the deceased's share must be worth less than precisely half of the full value; the value is reduced by the very fact that someone can still live there. For CTT, value means the price a buyer would pay in the open market on the day of death. It is hardly likely that a buyer (if one could be found) would pay as much as half of the vacant possession price for a half share, when there is a stranger still living in the house.

The result is that the proper value of the half-share (in the case of a joint tenancy or a tenancy in common held in equal shares) is half the vacant possession value, less something for the mere fact of it being held jointly. The £19,250 for half the vacant possession value might well be depressed to £17,500 on this account. There is no rigid formula that applies to this aspect of the valuation, and it is very difficult to arrive at a figure because, in practice, shares in joint tenancies in ordinary houses are hardly ever sold. Nevertheless, the expert valuer should be able to decide on a figure. Some valuation officers do not readily accept this basis of the value of the share in a house held by the deceased jointly with someone else, but it is correct.

Finally, account must be taken of any mortgage debt outstanding. Suppose that it is £2,000; then the deceased's share of this debt would normally be half, that is £1,000. The result would be that the value of the deceased's share of the house less the mortgage debt would be £17,500 minus £1,000, that is £16,500.

Matthew, however, was not involved in the problem of valuing a share in a house jointly held, because he knew that the house was in Mrs Blake's name alone. If Matthew had been uncertain whether the house was in her name alone or a joint ownership and there was no declaration of trust or other evidence of joint ownership among Mrs Blake's documents, he would now have enquired of the building society which held the title deeds.

There was a mortgage on the house, on which there was about £1,200 to be paid, according to a statement from the building society which Matthew had found in Mrs Blake's papers. The statement gave the position as it was on the previous 1 October, and it would be necessary, Matthew knew, to obtain an exact figure showing the position at the date of his mother-in-law's death. He wrote this letter to the building society:

14 Twintree Avenue
Minford, Surrey

9 January 1983

Dear Sir,

Re: Mary Josephine Blake deceased

I am an executor of the will of the late Mary Josephine Blake, who died on
5 January 1983; my co-executor is her son, Robert Anthony Blake.

Mrs Blake owned the house where she lived: The Firs, Willow Lane,
Minford, on which there is an outstanding mortgage with your society. The
reference number is AME716. Please let me know exactly how much capital
was outstanding on the mortgage at the date of death, and also the amount of
interest due up to that date.

I do not appear to have any record of the date on which the mortgage was
made. Please let me know this.

Yours faithfully,

Matthew J. Seaton

There had been little discussion so far about whether Mrs Blake's son
Mark, to whom she had left the house in her will, would continue to live
there, or whether it would be sold. What was to happen eventually could
be decided later on.

stocks and shares

Matthew next turned his attention to the question of finding out the value
of another item which made up his mother-in-law's property: the stocks
and shares.

(In this section of the book, the company names have been taken merely to
illustrate the workings of administering an estate, to give an air of reality.
The prices and dividends, and other figures are in no way intended to reflect
the actual performance of the shares over the period covered.)

In the deed box, together with the will, Matthew had found the stock and share certificates for the various holdings, namely:

£550 ordinary stock in ICI plc
£1,390 8 per cent preference stock in Unilever plc
£680 ordinary stock in The Metal Box plc
£2,000 10 per cent Treasury stock 1992
890 ordinary 25p shares in Shell Transport and Trading plc
1,460 ordinary 25p shares in Courtaulds plc
£2,355 Norwich Corporation 3 per cent Redeemable Stock
3,000 ordinary 25p shares in Westland Aircraft plc
2,000 ordinary 25p shares in Parker Knoll plc
15,000 ordinary 25p shares in Stonehill Holdings plc

Matthew had already made a rough calculation of what those items were worth on the date of death, by looking up the closing prices in the paper. Now it became necessary to work it out exactly, and in accordance with the accepted formula for valuing shares for CTT. This formula applies to stocks and shares which are bought and sold on the London Stock Exchange, and which are therefore quoted there. The shares of all the well-known large companies, and a great number of others as well, are quoted on the London Stock Exchange, as are war stock and numerous other government securities and similar investments, but not defence bonds.

On any particular day, there are sales of shares in nearly all the big concerns, and the prices often vary, depending on the prevailing circumstances. At any one time there are two prices quoted – the higher is that at which people buy and the lower at which people sell. The closing prices are the two prevailing prices of the share at the time in the afternoon when the stock exchange closed for the day; they are usually different from the highest or the lowest price at which the shares were quoted on that day.

the value of the holding
To work out the value which is officially recognised for probate purposes, it is necessary to know the closing prices on the day before the deceased's death. The *Stock Exchange Daily Official List*, a daily publication, gives the previous day's closing prices, the required figures, in a concise way. If the death was at the weekend, prices from the official list for the friday or for the monday may be used, and the executor may mix the friday and monday prices to his (that is, the estate's) advantage.

Not many people have ready access to the *Stock Exchange Daily Official*

List. The local reference library may take it, and a very large branch of a bank may take it. If you telephone your bank manager, quoting the securities you wish to value, he will be able to find out and let you know the closing prices for each share for the date of the death in question. If there is a long list, it is probably better to write to the bank. Alternatively, a stockbroker would be able to provide this information quite easily, either on the telephone in the case of a few quotations, or by letter if there are more.

Matthew decided to buy a copy of the official list for 5 January, to make the valuation. He wrote to Production Control, The Stock Exchange, St. Alphage House, Fore Street, London EC2, enclosing £2.50. The list, which was a 90-page book, came four days later. He found that seven of the companies in which he was interested were quoted in the section of the *Daily Official List* headed 'Commercial, Industrial'; the Shell shares were classified as being 'Oil'; Norwich Corporation was listed under Corporation and County stocks and the 'gilt-edged' Treasury stock came under British Funds.

In each case, Matthew found the two prices quoted. He was then able to adopt the official formula to work out the value of each for probate purposes. The formula is this: take as the figure a price which is one quarter up from the lower to the high figure. If the two figures in the quotation column of the *Stock Exchange Daily Official List* are, for instance 100p and 104p, then you take 101p as the value; if the two prices are 245p and 255p, then you take 247.5p as the value. The prices quoted in the official list are often prices for every £1 of stock held, or for every share held; the nominal value of a share may be 20p, 25p, £1, or any one of many other amounts.

Matthew prepared a complete table showing the share values. It looked like this:

Amount held	Description	Prices quoted	$^1/_4$ up from lower	Value of holding
		p	p	£
1,460	Courtaulds plc Ord	47–67	52	859.20
3,550	Imperial Chemical Industries plc Ord Stk	285–305	290	10,295.00
680	Metal Box plc Ord Stk	180–210	187.5	1,290.00
2,000	Parker Knoll plc Ord	110–130	115	2,300.00
15,000	Stonehill Holdings plc	61–65 xd	62	9,300.00
1,390	Unilever plc Ord 8% 2nd Cum Prf Stk	56–66	58.5	813.15
£2,000	Treasury 10% Stock 1992	82–84	82.5	1,650.00
3,000	Westland Aircraft plc Ord	122–132	124.5	3,735.00
890	Shell Transport & Trading plc Ord (Reg.)	392–412	402	3,577.80
2,355	Norwich Corp 3% Red Stk	18–22	19	447.45
				34,267.60

xd ex-dividend price

So the stocks and shares turned out to be worth, on the date of death, 34,267.60.

Matthew had now set about valuing all the securities he had been able to find belonging to his mother-in-law on the day of her death. (He made a note to remember that he would later have to account to the Inland Revenue for any income from the securities which he received while he was administering the estate.) There was not, apparently, any money in unit trusts. Unit trusts are also a common feature of the investment scene. To fix a value for these, an executor should write to the managers of the unit trust in question, to obtain a letter stating the value at the date of death.

Although older certificates are still quite valid, all companies whose shares are quoted on the Stock Exchange are now registered with the words 'Public Limited Company' or 'plc' at the end of the name. Private companies, whose shares are not quoted on the Stock Exchange (and which cannot be freely sold) still have the word 'Limited' or 'Ltd' at the end of their name.

Valuing shares in a private company not quoted on the Stock Exchange requires expert help, as a rule. Sometimes the secretary or accountant of the company concerned can state the price at which shares have recently changed hands, and this may be accepted for probate purposes. If not, a detailed and possibly difficult negotiation of value may have to be under taken and unless the shares are of comparatively small value, it would be worthwhile to get an accountant to handle the matter.

'ex-dividend'

Matthew noticed that the price for Stonehill Holdings plc had the letters xc beside it, which means that the price was quoted 'ex-dividend'. This means that if the shares are sold, the seller will receive the next dividend on these shares, not the buyer. The price the buyer pays is therefore lower than he would otherwise pay, to the extent of the dividend he is foregoing. This is because the company prepares the actual dividend cheques in advance in favour of the owner at that time, so if the shares are sold before the company sends out the cheque on the day the dividend is due, it will still go to the seller. This usually happens about six weeks before the date for payment of dividends.

In this case, the share's price went ex-dividend on 4 January 1983, so Matthew made a note to expect a dividend cheque towards the end of February. Because the price does not therefore reflect the full value of the shares, the dividend must be included as another asset in Matthew's list. He found out, by phoning the registrar of the company that the dividend to be paid on the shares was 1.715p each, so he calculated that the dividend would be £257.75. This would have to be included as a separate asset in the Inland Revenue account of Mary Blake's estate.

pensions

Amongst the private papers, Matthew found a description of the pension scheme operated by his late father-in-law's former employers, an engineering company. This was a contributory pension scheme under which he had received a pension until his death and which then provided a pension for Mrs Blake for the rest of her life. This pension had been half of the pension which her husband had been receiving. There was only one point arising out of the scheme which was strictly relevant to the administration of Mrs Blake's estate: the proportion of the month's pension due up to the date of her death. Matthew wrote this letter to the secretary of the pension fund:

14 Twintree Avenue
Minford, Surrey

15 January 1983

To: The Secretary, Staff Pension Scheme,
Minford Engineering Co Ltd,
Minford Lane, Surrey.

Dear Sir,

Re: Mary Josephine Blake deceased

You will be sorry to hear that Mrs Blake of The Firs, Willow Lane, Minford, died on 5 January. She was, as you know, receiving a widow's pension from the fund administered by you.

Her son, Mr Robert Anthony Blake, is one of the executors of her will, and I am the other. Please let me know the amount of Mrs Blake's pension due up to the date of her death.

Please also confirm that no capital sum is due to the estate under your pension scheme.

Yours faithfully,

Matthew Seaton

Employers' occupational pension schemes, which provide for the payment of a pension to a former member of the company's staff, vary in form and detail. Many are based on the employee's final salary; in some, the pension is calculated according to the contributions made to the pension fund by the company and by the member during the years in which he was employed by the company. This had been the basis of the pension which Herbert Blake had been receiving during his years of retirement. The scheme then went on to provide for the payment of a further pension to the widow of a pensioner, this being a proportion (in this case half) of the earlier pension. In these circumstances, no other payment, such as a capital payment to the executors, was due under the scheme.

Quite often a pension scheme provides that a capital sum should become payable on the death of one of its members. For instance, if a member were to die while still an employee, that is before retirement, the scheme might provide for the return of the contributions which had been made over the years by the member, and from which he has, in the event, derived no benefit, because he did not survive to collect his pension. If the lump sum that represents this return of contributions were part of the deceased's estate, it would have to be declared for CTT. However, in most schemes nowadays it would be paid 'at the trustees' discretion' and not be subject to CTT. Such schemes provide that the trustees may select who is to receive the capital sum (but they are bound by the rules of the particular scheme, and some are quite restrictive). They may pay it all to the widow or they may share it between any number of dependants or pay it to the executors as part of the estate. If they pay it to the widow or to the dependants, the money forms no part of the deceased's estate. As a result, the discretionary payment to a widow or dependant is not subject to CTT.

Whatever the circumstances, it is probably best, where the deceased belonged to a pension scheme, to get a letter from the secretary of the pension fund to confirm the exact position regarding what the estate (as distinct from a dependant) is entitled to receive under the scheme. Even if it is only the proportion of the pension due for the last few days of life, a letter should be obtained to provide written confirmation for the purpose of CTT.

Matthew's mother-in-law had also been receiving the state old age pension, or national insurance retirement pension, as it is properly called. Matthew found the pension book and noticed that she had not drawn her pension for the three weeks up to the date of her death.

As soon as he could, Matthew visited the Minford office of the Department of Health and Social Security. He took with him: his mother-in-law's pension book; the death certificate which is specially provided, free of charge, for national insurance purposes by the registrar of births and deaths; and the marriage certificate of Mr and Mrs Blake. There were only two matters which had to be dealt with at the social security office: the arrears of Mrs Blake's retirement pension and the death grant in respect of Mrs Blake's death.

Mrs Blake had been receiving the usual state retirement pension, based on her late husband's national insurance contributions up to his retirement at the age of 65. Matthew was told that the arrears of pension, as well as the full pension for the week in which death took place, would be paid to the executors. Pensions are paid on a specified day each week, for the week ahead. If a person collects the pension on thursday and then dies on the following monday, his estate would not be liable to refund any part of that week's pension. Where a person received the pension monthly or quarterly in arrears, or paid directly into a bank account, the death should be reported to the local office of the Department of Health and Social Security who will adjust the payment accordingly.

Matthew handed in his mother-in-law's pension book. The sum due for arrears of pension would be paid to him and to Robert, as the executors, after probate had been obtained. The arrears of pension formed part of Mrs Blake's estate; it would have to be declared for CTT and included in the probate papers.

Next, Matthew enquired about the state death grant. This grant depends on the relevant national insurance contributions record, and on the date of birth. In Mrs Blake's case, there was not likely to be any difficulty or delay in obtaining payment of the full death grant of £30. For some cases, where an insufficient number of contributions has been paid or credited in the past, there can be a payment of part of the grant. Matthew completed the claim form to obtain the death grant. The death grant is not liable for CTT, and does not have to be included as an item of the deceased's property to be declared in the probate papers.

The Consumer Publication *What to do when someone dies* gives a detailed account of national insurance grants, allowances and pensions that may be due after a death, and how to obtain them.

income tax

Income tax is calculated on a person's total income in the tax year, April to April. PAYE works so that tax is deducted week by week, or month by month, on the assumption that the taxpayer will go on having income throughout the year. If he dies during the year, the PAYE assumptions are upset, because the taxpayer did not live to receive the income throughout the tax year, and often a tax repayment is due. Also, if the taxpayer was not liable for tax at the standard rate, because his income did not reach that level, he may be entitled to a tax repayment if some of his income is taxed at the standard rate before he gets it; dividends from shares fall within this category. It is therefore usual for personal representatives to explain the situation fully to the local inspector of taxes, and if necessary to go and see him about the repayment that may be due because too much income tax was suffered by the deceased during the tax year in which he died. Although tax is only claimed on the amount of income due up to the date of death, tax allowances (such as a married man's personal allowance) are granted for the full year, even if the death took place early in the tax year.

Now Matthew wrote to the local inspector of taxes.

14 Twintree Avenue
Minford, Surrey

17 January 1983

To: HM Inspector of Taxes
High Street
Minford

Dear Sir,

Re: Mary Josephine Blake deceased

The tax affairs of the above-named have, I believe, been dealt with in your district, under reference B 246537. Mrs Blake of The Firs, Willow Lane, Minford died on 5 January 1983. Her son Robert Anthony Blake, of Wringapeak Farm, Woody Bay, North Devon and I are the executors of her will, and we are in the process of applying for a grant of probate.

The only income which Mrs Blake was receiving up to the date of her death consisted of: pension from her late husband's former employers' pension fund (which was subject to PAYE); her state retirement pension; and dividends from various investments. I enclose a list of them showing dividends received from 6 April to the date of death. There may be a repayment due to Mrs Blake in respect of PAYE deducted (and dividends taxed by deduction at the standard rate) for the period up to the date of her death in the current tax year. You will probably be able to calculate this without further information from me, but if there is any information you require for the purpose, please let me know. I shall need to know the amount of the repayment for probate purposes, so I look forward to hearing from you.

Yours faithfully,

Matthew Seaton

contents of house and cash

The next item requiring valuation was the furniture and effects. This includes furniture in the house, household goods of all kinds, jewellery, clothes, a car and all personal possessions. It is not necessary to prepare a complete list, nor state the respective values of different kinds of articles; they can all be lumped together.

The make and age of the car are the principal factors which affect its value; its condition is a minor consideration. A study of the prices being asked for secondhand cars by local garages or dealers will give an indication of the value, to within about £50.

The remaining articles are not so easily valued. It is better to put a separate valuation on items of particular value, such as things worth more than about £100, when making a calculation of the total value of the effects. This might apply, for example, to a particular piece of jewellery, or a picture, especially if its value is reasonably well established, because it was recently purchased, for instance, or because it had been valued recently by an expert, perhaps for insurance.

Matthew was not sure whether any of his mother-in-law's jewellery was worth a lot. He put into a box her wedding ring, a gold watch, several necklaces, one of which seemed to be made of gold with a ruby pendant, a pearl tie-pin (perhaps itself an heirloom) and the rather beautiful diamond and garnet brooch mentioned in the will. The local jeweller made a careful list of these items and asked Matthew whether he needed the valuation for probate or insurance purposes. For probate purposes, only the intrinsic value of the precious metal or stones is taken into consideration, not the workmanship of the items. That is why the total value of Mrs Blake's jewellery came to only £137. Matthew had to pay a valuation fee of £6.75. The jeweller gave him a receipt for this amount and the official valuation certificate. Matthew would include the valuation fee in the administration account.

The other item Matthew had to consider was the paintings. He had found, among the papers, the insurance policy for the home and contents and, with it, the latest endorsement for the renewal and review of the sum insured. In the contents section items above £300 had to be specifically mentioned. In that section, the paintings were specifically shown as £600, £500, and £400 respectively. Matthew made a note of them.

general valuation
More difficult to fix is a value for the great bulk of the household furniture and effects. How do you decide what the tables, chairs, beds, linen, cups and saucers, carpets, TV set, clothes and all the rest of it are actually worth? You have to decide what price they would get if sold on the day of death. This means in practice what they would fetch at an auction. Of course, the secondhand value of the great majority of items is considerably less than the cost when new. For CTT, you do not consider the cost of replacement, but the price they would fetch if sold secondhand. The capital taxes office of the Inland Revenue does not expect you to provide an expert's valuation,

nor one that is accurate to within a few pounds, but a valuation that is honest and sensible, and says what the executor really thinks the items are worth.

This was Matthew's approach to the problem. He spent a saturday afternoon going round the house with his brother-in-law Mark, discussing what was in the house. Where necessary they discussed when, where, and by whom, various items had been bought, in order to exclude items which belonged to Mark already. Matthew made a few notes as they went along. When they had finished, he totted it all up. It came to more than his first guess. The figure he finally arrived at for the furniture and effects was £1,645, plus £1,320 for the car.

One other article needed special consideration: the dishwasher. Matthew found that his mother-in-law was buying it on hire purchase, and there were four more monthly payments of £11.55 each to be paid. How should this be dealt with in his valuation of Mrs Blake's property? Strictly speaking, the dishwasher itself was not something which belonged to Mrs Blake; it still belonged to the finance company. What she had owned – and which consequently had passed to the executors – was a right to become the owner of the dishwasher, when the remaining instalments had been paid, together with a right to use the dishwasher in the meantime. But it is not necessary to go through the solemn process of trying to value something so esoteric as a right of this kind. It is sufficient to take a commonsense attitude by valuing the article as if it had been part of what the deceased owned, along with everything else, and then to treat the instalments still to be paid as a debt due from her. This is what Matthew did about the dishwasher. His estimate of its current secondhand value, which he put at £90, was included as part of the £1,645, the value of the furniture and effects. The four outstanding hire purchase instalments of £11.55 each he would include as a debt of £46.20. He ignored the fact that these instalments were not actually due at the date of death, but only over the next four months. Matthew would have applied the same process of valuation if it had been the car, or any other articles, which Mrs Blake had been paying for on hire purchase.

Matthew now considered the simplest asset of them all: cash. In Mary Blake's handbag, in the drawer of her desk, and in one or two other places, Matthew found odd sums of cash. Altogether this came to £18.40.

debts

If anyone had owed money to Mrs Blake, Matthew would have included it in the list of property declared for CTT. Any sums of money which are owed to the deceased count as assets. They are debts due to the estate.

Debts due from the deceased have to be listed, too. Any money which he owes reduces what he owns for the purpose of calculating his total property: the liabilities are deducted from the assets. These debts can consist of almost anything: rates, fuel bills, tax, telephone account, amounts due on credit cards or credit accounts, hire purchase debts, an overdraft, for example. In addition, the funeral expenses must be deducted.

Mrs Blake had a few debts. Matthew found an unpaid bill for gas, which his mother-in-law had perhaps forgotten. There was a telephone account as well, and the hire purchase for the dishwasher. In the course of the first few weeks after his mother-in-law's death. Matthew received two more bills, and these he added to the list: a bill for servicing the car, and another for some wines and spirits. Matthew assembled the invoices for these items, and wrote a short note to the companies and organisations who were owed money, explaining that they would be paid soon after probate was granted.

finding the creditors

It can happen that a personal representative has reason to wonder whether all the deceased's debts have come to his notice. For this situation, there is a special procedure, which involves advertising for creditors. The personal representative puts an advertisement in the *London Gazette* and a daily newspaper announcing that all claims against the estate have to be made by a date not less than two months ahead. There is a standard way of setting out the notice, which has to include the name of the person who has died, the date of death, and the names and address of the person to whom notice of a claim is to be given. Where this is done in the official way, the personal representative is quite safe in dealing with the estate on the basis of the debts known to him on the date by which claims have to be made, according to the advertisement. If a personal representative does not advertise for creditors in this way, there is always a danger, however slight, that after he has parted with the assets to the beneficiaries, some unknown creditor appears on the scene and justifiably claims that the deceased owed him money. If that were to happen, the personal representative would have to pay the debt out of his own pocket, if he had not advertised for creditors. He could probably claim the money back from the beneficiaries, but even that might be difficult.

applying for probate forms

Matthew knew that it would probably be a few weeks before all the information about valuing the estate would be complete and before he could proceed to the next stage: applying for the grant of probate. But it was not too soon to write for the forms that he would be needing for his application. Matthew had received a booklet when he had registered the death, which contained the addresses of the district registries of the probate registry, from which forms could be obtained. He wrote to the Probate Personal Application Department, Principal Registry of the Family Division, 5th Floor, Golden Cross House, Duncannon Street, London WC2N 4JF (telephone: 01-214 3015 or 01-214 3116). He asked for the forms required to enable him to make a personal application for a grant of probate. (Had Mary Blake not left a will, he would have asked for the forms relevant to an application for a grant of letters of administration.)

It is possible to write or telephone for the forms to a local district probate registry or subregistry; they are in

Bangor (telephone: 2410)
Birmingham (telephone: 236 4560/6263)
Bodmin (telephone: 2279)
Brighton (telephone: 684071)
Bristol (telephone: 23915/24619)
Carlisle (telephone: 21751)
Carmarthen (telephone: 6238)
Chester (telephone: 20997)
Exeter (telephone: 74515)
Gloucester (telephone: 22585)
Ipswich (telephone: 53724)
Lancaster (telephone: 65911)
Leeds (telephone: 31505)
Leicester (telephone: 546117)
Lincoln (telephone: 23648)

Liverpool (telephone: 236 8264)
Llandaff (telephone: 562422)
Maidstone (telephone: 51737)
Manchester (telephone: 834 4319)
Middlesbrough (telephone: 244770)
Newcastle-upon-Tyne (telephone: 328543 ext 260/268)
Norwich (telephone: 26648)
Nottingham (telephone: 51337)
Oxford (telephone: 41163/44356)
Peterborough (telephone: 62802)
Sheffield (telephone: 29920/78317)
Stoke-on-Trent (telephone: 23736)
Winchester (telephone: 3046/63771)
York (telephone: 24210)

finance for CTT

Matthew next considered how to raise the money needed to pay the CTT. In his first rough calculation he had estimated that the duty would be around £9,000. In the light of the way the valuation of the property was proceeding, it seemed likely that his first estimate had been too low. He could see that the estate would in fact come to over £80,000; the tax would be around £11,000.

In theory, the executors are faced with an odd dilemma. On the one hand, no bank or insurance company which holds money belonging to the estate may confidently hand any of it over to the executors until a grant of probate is obtained and produced to them; the probate is the only authority which can allow them to part with the money. On the other hand, the executors cannot obtain a grant of probate until they have actually paid the CTT, or at least most of it. How can they pay the tax, without being able to get their hands on the wherewithal to pay it?

from National Savings
If there are funds in the National Savings Bank, these can be used to pay the CTT. So can national savings certificates and premium bonds, also british savings bonds, and government stocks on the section of the National Savings Stock Register kept by the Department for National Savings, and money from save-as-you-earn contracts. A special system operates between the personal application department of the probate registry and the Department for National Savings which enables this to be done. The executor has to explain that he needs to use the national savings monies for paying the tax, when he first visits the probate registry; he will be given a note, on probate registry notepaper, showing that personal application has been made and stating the amount of capital transfer tax payable. He should send this to the appropriate office of the Department for National Savings, together with the savings bank account book, the savings certificates, the bond books or investment certificates, or the save-as-you-earn proposal acceptance form or the premium savings bonds. For these last two, a repayment application form is also necessary, which can be obtained from most post offices or banks.

The Department for National Savings will then send a cheque for the tax direct to the probate registry, and the balance of the national savings monies will be made available to the executors after probate is obtained. The balance of any save-as-you-earn money that remains after tax has been paid, will not earn any interest or enhancement prior to being repaid when the grant of probate is produced.

other arrangements for CTT money

Generally, assets cannot be dealt with before there is a grant. But if the person who died had a building society account, it is possible that the society will release money from the account for the purpose of providing finance for CTT (and probate fees). A cheque will be issued not to the executors but made payable to the Inland Revenue for the CTT and to the Paymaster General for the probate fees.

If the person who died had a Girobank account, the executors may, subject to satisfactory identification, borrow for the purpose of paying CTT, so that a grant of probate may be obtained. The borrowing is limited to solvent estates and to the amount of the credit balance in the deceased's account.

arrangements with the bank

Mrs Blake had not had a building society account (and even if she had, there might not have been enough in it for around £11,000 tax, plus around £400 probate fees).

The obvious place it appeared to Matthew to approach was the bank where Mary Blake had kept her account. So he went to see the manager of the branch, the Barminster Bank at Minford. The manager agreed to lend Matthew and Robert the money for paying the CTT. Banks usually do, unless the deceased had a sizeable overdraft when he died and the bank fears that it might not be met. In such a case it can be useful if the executor can point out that there are, for example, share certificates (perhaps even lodged at the bank) of at least the value of the overdraft. The executor may be asked what shares will be sold and may have to agree that the actual sale will be carried out by the bank's broker and the overdraft paid off first, before the executor gets the rest of the proceeds.

Matthew did not have any difficulties in the bank manager agreeing a loan limit of £13,000. This would easily cover all probate fees and tax, which seemed prudent to Matthew, even if he would not need to draw to the full extent of the limit. (He knew that, because about half the value of the estate was represented by the house, the CTT payable on this could be postponed.)

It was arranged that an account should be immediately opened at that branch in the name of the two executors, and would be known as the executorship account. For the time being, the account was to be without funds, but Matthew would be sent a cheque book in the course of a few days. When the time came to pay the duty, Matthew and Robert would sign a cheque for the necessary amount, and the bank would meet it.

It was also arranged that a separate loan account should be opened which would fund the CTT and probate fees, specifically. The appropriate amounts would be transferred from the loan account to the executorship account to meet the cheques for CTT and probate fees. Where these items are kept identifiable from the amounts drawn on the executorship account, by prior arrangement with the bank, the interest payable is deducted from the income in the estate, for income tax purposes, for the period of administration.

When, later on, the grant of probate had been obtained (but not before), the executors would be in a position to transfer the money in Mrs Blake's own account at the bank into the executorship account. This could then partly reduce the loan account balance, which would be completely paid off when the insurance monies were received and some of the shares sold. In the meantime, the executors would have to pay interest on the whole amount outstanding, even though at the same branch there was another account, which was temporarily untouchable but which really belonged to the executors as well. Sometimes it is possible to arrange with the bank manager that, until probate is obtained, the two accounts shall be treated as one, so that the amount standing to the credit of the deceased's account may be set against the overdraft on the executorship account. But this cannot always be arranged, and there is no way of insisting that it should. Indeed, there is not even a way of insisting that the bank should provide an overdraft to pay the CTT.

It is often possible to arrange with the bank for the balance of an account at death to be placed on deposit in the deceased's name. The interest figure which, in due course, would be added, would then have to be included in the income tax return for the administration period.

finalising the valuation

It was not long before Matthew began to receive letters providing a precise valuation of the assets. He heard from the Department for National Savings about the savings bank account and the savings certificates; he heard from the insurance company that the policy money and the profits to be paid amounted to a total of £4,068.97.

The bank manager had handed a letter to Matthew when he went to discuss the CTT, and this letter stated the exact sum which stood to the credit of Mrs Blake's current account at the bank at the date of death: £193.52. The bank account was frozen as soon as the manager had been told of Mrs Blake's death. No further payment would be made out of the account either for cheques signed by Mrs Blake but not presented till after her death, or on banker's orders.

Matthew heard from the local inspector of taxes, who stated that a tax repayment would probably be due to his mother-in-law's estate, but required a tax form to be completed first. This did not worry Matthew because he knew that for the CTT form he could put in an estimate of this figure, and notify the correct figure to the CTT office at a later date.

Matthew heard from the building society about the mortgage on the house. He was told that the amount outstanding on the mortgage on 5 January 1983 was £1,168.44. He was also told the date of the mortgage, which he had not been able to find in Mrs Blake's records, but which he would need for the probate papers.

Then he heard from the secretary of the pension fund. There was £22.30 due for the proportion of Mrs Blake's pension for the part of the month of January during which she was alive. No other sum was due to the estate from the pension fund.

Within a month of Mary Blake's death, Matthew had collected all the necessary information about the estate of his mother-in-law. The funeral account, amounting to £410.50 was amongst documents he collected together. Matthew was now able to complete the forms which would enable him to apply for a grant of probate.

filling in probate forms

Matthew had received the probate forms from the personal application department of the probate registry in London, and it would be with that department at Duncannon Street in London that Matthew would be making all further arrangements. Had he lived in the provinces, he would have obtained the forms from, and would be making all further arrangements with, the nearest district registry of the probate registry. The procedure, after the forms are completed, can vary in minor respects not only between London and the provincial towns, but also between different district registries.

In straightforward cases, there is a system which enables the matter to go through mainly by post and with only one visit to the probate registry. The executor has first of all to complete and send in the forms, so that they can be checked and the amounts of probate fees and CTT assessed; the registry officials prepare the document which the executor will then have to swear to be true. It is necessary for the executor to attend personally at the probate registry for this. If all is in order, an appointment is made, by post, for the executor to attend to swear the papers within about three to five weeks, but sometimes there is a considerably longer delay.

The forms which Matthew had received by post from the probate registry were these:

form PR48: an explanation of the procedure on making a personal application
form PR48A: a list of local probate offices
form PR83: a form of instructions for probate
Cap form 44: *Return for estate duty/capital transfer tax*
Cap form 37B: *Schedule of real and leasehold/immovable property*
Cap form 40: *Statement of stocks and shares.*

form PR83
To complete form 83 was quite simple. It contained panels in which Matthew gave the required information. Firstly the form asked at which office the applicant wished to attend. Matthew put London. Then it asked for particulars about the deceased. Next Matthew completed particulars of the applicants, himself and his brother-in-law. (The first named would be

the one with whom the personal application department of the probate registry would normally correspond, unless specially requested to do otherwise.)

The form had a space for naming any executors who were not applying for probate because they were dead, or did not wish to act as executor. If they did not wish to act but might apply to do so later, the probate office sends an official 'power reserved' letter which the non-acting executor has to sign.

Matthew had to give details of the surviving relatives. There were also spaces for information about illegitimate children (where a will is not being proved by an executor).

Matthew found that he did not have to sign form PR83. This was because the form is used by the probate registry as the basis for another form, and an oath, which they prepare. These contain the same particulars, more or less, as form 83, but express them in the stipulated legal language and the oath is eventually sworn by the executors.

form 44

The rest of the forms were mainly concerned with providing details of the property which the deceased had left. Form 44 is the main one. It is used as the basis for the preparation by the probate registry of the actual document which the personal representatives will have to sign: the Inland Revenue account. In some cases, for instance where the gross estate is les than £25,000, there is no need for an Inland Revenue account, but the form 44 still has to be completed.

There is space on form 44 to fill in details of each of the assets which comprise the deceased's estate. The form contains reasonably clear instructions about what has to be included and how to fill it in, but the form itself is confusing. The main part begins on page 3, under the headng 'Property of the deceased in the United Kingdom', and it is best to turn to that part first.

Matthew had by him all the letters and memoranda which he had obtained about the value of the various assets. Item 1 on page 3 of the form was for British Savings Bonds, National Development Bonds, War Loan and other government securities. Matthew could have found a valuation for War Loan and Savings Bonds in the *Stock Exchange Daily Official List*; Defence Bonds are worth their face value. As it happened, Mrs Blake had none of these, so there was nothing to fill in there.

Item 2 was for savings certificates. Matthew wrote 'see letter' alongside, as he meant to attach to the form 44 the actual letter from the Department for National Savings showing the value of the savings certificates. The figure he wrote in the column headed 'Principal value at date of death' was £942.50. Matthew kept a note of the reference number on the letter from the Department for National Savings, as he would need to quote it when it came to cashing the savings certificates after probate had been obtained.

Item 3 was for details of premium bonds. These are worth their face value, so Matthew filled in £1,500 in the same column underneath the £942.50.

Item 4 on the form said: 'Other stocks, shares or investments including unit trusts'. If Mrs Blake had owned just one or two lots of shares, Matthew could have written the details of them on form 44. But there were ten lots of stocks and shares here, and therefore not quite enough room to give the required particulars of them all. One of the other forms he had been sent was specially designed for providing these details, so Matthew used it.

form 40

Form 40 is buff-coloured and ruled into columns to enable the necessary data about the stocks and shares to be set out in tabular form. When completed, form 40 looked rather like the valuation which Matthew had prepared for his own benefit, but rearranged in the order in which they appear in the official list.

The form was headed 'Statement of stocks and shares etc'. The first (and main) column in it asked for a full description of the class of share or stock. It was necessary to specify the type of stock or shares, as well as the name of the company. Do not worry if you do not know the company registration number.

The next column asked for the unit of quotation. This meant the unit of the stock or shares, the value of which was quoted on the stock exchange. In the case of stock, the unit of quotation is often £1, but not necessarily so. In the case of shares, the unit of quotation is one share, as a rule. The exact type of denomination of stock and shares can be found very simply by looking at the certificates.

The next column in form 40 was headed 'Holding – No. of Shares or amount of Stock'. This asked for the quantity which the deceased had held of the investment concerned, measured in terms of so much of the unit of quotation, referred to in the previous column.

The next column asked for the market price at date of valuation, which means the date of death or the date nearest to it on which the *Stock*

Exchange Daily Official List was published. This is where the formula of the 'one quarter up' applies. Having found the quotations in the *Stock Exchange Daily Official List*, Matthew entered on the form the figure one quarter up from the lower price, as this was the recognised market value for the purpose of capital transfer tax.

The next column was headed: 'Source of Market Price if other than the Stock Exchange Official List for date of valuation'. Some shares are quoted on provincial stock exchanges. Shares in a private company (a family business, for example) are also not quoted on the Stock Exchange. Where this happens, it is sometimes difficult to establish an authoritative valuation of the shares, and professional assistance in arriving at an acceptable valuation is likely to be needed. In the normal case, such as Mary Blake's, the column does not apply and is left blank.

The last column to be completed on form 40 asked for the principal value at date of valuation. This was arrived at by multiplying the number of shares or the amount of stock by the market price at date of death.

Matthew completed form 40 with particulars of the ten holdings of stocks and shares which Mary Blake had owned. (By the price for the Stonehill Holdings shares, Matthew put 'xd', indicating that the price was quoted ex-dividend on the day concerned; the amount of the declared dividend, yet to be received, would have to be included later on in the form.) The total value came to £34,267.60 and this was the figure which he entered as item 4 on form 44, for 'Other stocks, shares and investments'.

form 44 again
He wrote the words 'See form 40' alongside item 4, to indicate where full details could be found of how the £34,267.60 was made up, and also wrote this figure in the column of form 44.

The fifth item to be listed on form 44 was cash. Matthew had collected and counted it, and it had come to £18.40, so that was the figure he entered. He had not considered it necessary to pay the actual notes and coins he had found belonging to his mother-in-law into the executorship bank account. It was quite in order to keep the cash to defray small expenses of the administration. But he made a note of everything he spent.

Item 6 on form 44 was: 'Cash at bank, namely at . . .'. Matthew wrote in: 'Barminster Bank, Minford' and filled in the amount – £193.52 – in the figures column.

The next item was: 'Money at SAVINGS BANKS or in BUILDING, CO-OPERATIVE or FRIENDLY SOCIETIES, including interest to date of death'. In Mrs Blake's case, there was merely the money in the National Savings Bank, so that was what Matthew wrote on the form and the amount including the interest on the money which had accrued up to the date of death: £389.20. Had there been any other assets of that category, money in a building society, for instance, a friendly society, or any savings bank, the procedure would have been the same.

Item 8 was for insurance policies. Where the form asked for the name of the company, Matthew filled in 'Bridstow Insurance Company', and the amount to be shown in the figures column was the amount to be paid in respect of the policy including bonuses. The letter from the insurance company had stated this amount: £4,068.97.

Item 9 was intended also for insurance policies, but this time for policies taken out by the deceased on someone else's life: someone who was still alive. Occasionally, a woman takes out a policy on the life of her husband, because she has a vital financial interest in his continued ability to earn money; an employer may insure in case of the death of a crucial employee, such as a sales director. In these and other ways, one sometimes finds a case of one person insuring someone else's life. Where this happens, the policy counts as an asset in the estate of the person who took out the policy, and the value to be shown is the surrender value at the date of death. This is something which the insurance company would give in a letter to the executors. Mrs Blake had no such policies.

Item 10 on form 44 referred to 'household and personal goods'. Matthew had already carefully valued them. The value of the car was £1,320, the jewellery had been valued at £137, the pictures were £1,500 and £1,645 was the value of the remaining items. He put the figure of £4,602 in the figures column of the form alongside item 10 without explanation; none was needed.

Item 11 asked for 'amounts due from employers'. The proportion of Mrs Blake's pension from her late husband's former employer's pension fund up to the date of her death amounted to £22.30. Matthew entered this amount on the form.

Item 12, 'other assets', was an omnibus item, the place to fill in details of almost anything not covered elsewhere. Matthew included three items here: the arrears of the state retirement pension, amounting to £47.07; and the estimated amount of the tax refund due from the Inland Revenue. He completed this part of the form with these bare details, and did not add any particulars, nor include supporting evidence. The third item was the dividend on the shares quoted 'ex-dividend'. All Matthew wrote here was

'Dividend declared at the date of death 1.715p per share on 15,000 shares in Stonehill Holdings plc – see form 40' and he filled in a figure for this item of £257.75. He would be receiving a dividend warrant for the amount shortly. He had not yet told the company of Mary Blake's death, so the warrant would be made out to Mary Blake.

Item 13 covered a civil servant's death benefit, the capital sum paid to the estate of permanent civil servants if they die in service. Mary Blake had not been a civil servant, so there was nothing to fill in there.

Item 14 only applies where the deceased owned a business; Mary Blake did not, and Matthew ignored the item.

Item 15 was the one for the house. It asked about 'Freehold and leasehold property situated at . . .' Matthew completed the address of the house which Mrs Blake had owned and lived in: The Firs, Willow Lane, Minford. Alongside, he wrote his estimate of the value of the house: £45,000. He turned his attention to form 37B, referred to in item 15. It was headed: SCHEDULE OF REAL AND LEASEHOLD / IMMOVABLE PROPERTY.

form 37B
The form was designed to cover a great variety of properties, not only houses. Column 2 asked for a description of the property, and Matthew wrote its postal address. Column 3 asked for details of tenure; the answer was: freehold. If the property had been of leasehold tenure, the number of unexpired years of the lease should have been shown in column 3.

Column 4 applied to property that was let and as that did not apply to Matthew's case, he left it blank.

Column 5 covered agricultural land; Matthew left it blank.

The important question came in column 6; 'Value of property transferred . . .' which meant the capital value on the open market at the date of death. This was where Matthew filled in the figure £45,000. The outstanding amount of the mortgage debt is treated separately as a debt for CTT purposes, rather than an amount by which the value of the property is reduced. Only property which has a capital value has to be included for CTT. A tenancy of a house or flat normally has no capital value and nothing need be said about it in the probate forms.

At the bottom of the form were questions about timber, that is woodland; about any agreement with the district valuer (the local representative of the Inland Revenue on questions of property valuation) as to agreed values; whether any of the properties were unoccupied; about sales (of the house, for instance), past and future. Matthew answered 'No' to all but the last question which asked whether anything would be sold within one year. There he answered 'not yet known'.

He wrote the name of the deceased and her date of death at the top of the form, and form 37B was complete.

form 44 again

Pages 1 and 2 of the form 44 were devoted to further items of property which have to be included for probate purposes where they exist. None of them applied to Mrs Blake's estate. Item 1 was about settled property. A settlement is an arrangement whereby a person transfers some of his property (generally some investments) during his lifetime to trustees who are directed to pay the income from the investments to one person for a period, often for that person's life, and then to divide up the capital among others. Wealthy people often make a settlement on the marriage of one of their children, when it is called a marriage settlement. A similar sort of disposition of property can also be made in a person's will, but then it operates only after the death of the person who makes it. Mrs Blake had not been entitled to an interest under a settlement during her lifetime. Matthew therefore deleted the YES, leaving NO as the answer.

Item 2 on page 1 was about accumulations. This is something that could have arisen under a settlement if Mrs Blake had made one. Matthew felt it was unlikely that his mother-in-law had indulged in anything so sophisticated as making a settlement that would accumulate income and cease on her death, and therefore, as with item 1, the answer was NO.

Item 3 was about gifts. All gifts, irrespective of value, are supposed to be shown and details of the date, value, to whom given and address to be stated. Wedding presents do not usually count as a gift, however hefty they may be. For practical purposes, you can ignore Christmas presents and birthday presents within the normal limits; and although gifts in any one year under £3,000 are exempt from CTT, they should be listed. In fact, item 3 was a little confusing. It was divided into three questions, the first of which asked about gifts or settlements within seven years of death.

The period of seven years about which the form actually asks is a hangover from the old Estate Duty rules, which applied before CTT came into force. In fact, CTT is payable at rates dependent on what transfers were made within the last ten years, and also particularly during the last three years for which, though life-time gifts, the (higher) death rates apply, as explained earlier. (The only conceivable circumstance in which Estate

Duty rules are still relevant is on the death of a widow or widower who was the life-tenant under the trust of the will of a spouse who died prior to 1975.)

The other two questions under item 3 refer to gifts, dispositions and settlements to relatives only. For these purposes, a settlement is a gift which is not to one person absolutely and a disposition means any transfer of property whether for value or not. One usually puts 'NO – other than usual Christmas or birthday presents'.

It is not sufficient to give away your house if you make it a condition that you be allowed to live in the house for the rest of your life. Such an arrangement would fail to avoid liability for CTT on the house, even though you died more than ten years after the gift.

The personal representatives must enquire among those who are most likely to have received gifts, and only if everyone says 'no' should they answer NO on form 44, as Matthew did.

Item 4 was about policies of assurance. There are all sorts of insurance policies that can be taken out, apart from ordinary life or endowment policies, particulars of which would already have been shown in item 8 on page 3 of form 44. For example, some policies provide that the money shall be paid to a named relative, such as a daughter, rather than form part of the deceased's estate. Item 4 was concerned with any such policies on which the deceased had paid a premium within the last seven years. Matthew said: NO.

Item 5 was about nominations, that is property of any kind nominated by the deceased during his lifetime in favour of any person. (This procedure can no longer be used, but nominations already made remain valid.) For example, savings bank accounts, savings certificates and friendly society accounts could be nominated this way. They do not form part of the deceased's estate, and so do not pass through the hands of the personal representatives, but pass direct to the person to whom they are nominated. Nevertheless, they have to be declared for the purposes of CTT, and details must be included in item 5. There being none in Mary Blake's case, Matthew replied: NO.

Item 6 on form 44 was headed: 'Superannuation benefits'. It asked whether any sum of money or annuity became payable on the death to any person under a superannuation scheme. In Mary Blake's case, the answer to this was: NO. Sometimes, under an occupational pension scheme, a pension now becomes payable to a widow. If so, it is usual to attach a copy of the letter from the secretary of the staff pension scheme concerned.

Item 7 asked whether there was any property held jointly. Had there been a house held jointly, or a joint bank account, the answer would have been: YES. The purpose of the question, broadly speaking, is to find out the source of funds used to acquire the joint property; to determine what proportion of the purchase money actually came from the deceased's resources. This is often crucial in fixing the extent of CTT liability on the joint property.

For Matthew, completing item 7 on form 44 was easy. There was no jointly held property in Mary Blake's case, so Matthew simply replied: NO.

Page 6 (Account 2) of form 44 was for property which is physically outside the United Kingdom. A villa in Spain would have had to be included there; so would an interest in a business which was carried on abroad.

At the bottom of page 6 was a space for the signatures of the applicants, in this case Robert Blake and Matthew.

Page 5 of form 44 was for details of debts. Matthew had earlier assembled the bills which he had been able to find, for gas, telephone, wines and spirits, car service, and hire purchase on the dishwasher. In the left-hand column Matthew filled in particulars in each case of who was owed the money; in the next column – under 'Description of debt' – he stated what each was for: gas, telephone and so on; in the third column he filled in the amount of each debt. Matthew totalled the debts, and they came to £227.06. In the middle of the page was a space for details of the funeral expenses. Matthew inserted the name of the funeral directors and the amount of their bill – £410.50. There was then a space for the total of the debts and the funeral expenses, which in this case was £637.56.

At the bottom of the page was the space for details of a mortgage. This applied in Mary Blake's case, and Matthew filled in the details of the mortgage with the Minford Building Society, from whom he had obtained particulars. In the column alongside, he stated the amount of money which was outstanding at the date of death: £1,168.44.

Where a property is held jointly, the amount to be included as a debt is the deceased's share of the mortgage (normally half in the case of a joint tenancy).

Finally, the form asked for details of any business debt. This only applies where the deceased carried on a business himself. Matthew left the column blank.

sending off the forms

Matthew arranged a meeting with Robert, his brother-in-law and co-executor, and went carefully through the completed forms with him, and explained each item to him, to be sure he understood it and that it was accurately completed. He did and each was. Of the three forms which Matthew had completed, only form 44 needed to be signed.

Matthew would be posting the original of Mrs Blake's will to the probate registry, and thought that it should not be sent without his first taking a photo-copy. Then he bundled into the large envelope, which had come with the forms, these documents: the will, death certificate, form PR83, form 44, form 37B and form 40. To form 44 he attached the original letter from the Department for National Savings about the savings certificates. He enclosed a short covering letter listing the enclosures. It is important that none of the forms or letters are clipped or pinned to the will. Matthew checked this before finally sealing the envelope and sending it, by recorded delivery, to the personal application department of the probate registry in London.

If there had been any queries on the forms, Matthew would probably have received a letter from the registry asking him to attend there. The difficulties would then have been cleared, and an appointment sub-sequently made for Robert Blake and him to go to the registry to swear the papers. As it happened, there were no queries, and Matthew eventually received a form from the registry, which asked him and Robert Blake to come to Golden Cross House at a stated time on a particular day, 10.30 a.m. on 25 February.

He was told, in the letter, to bring his glasses if he needed them for reading, and the fee.

fees

The probate fees are charges made by the probate registry for dealing with the papers and issuing the grant of probate. They fall into two parts. There is the normal court fee, which is paid in all cases, where the net estate is not under £25,000, including those where a solicitor takes out the grant. Then there is an additional, departmental, fee which has to be paid where the grant is taken out without a solicitor, through the personal application department. It covers the extra work involved in the registry where the personal representatives are not legally represented. Both of these fees are calculated on the amount of the net estate, as declared for the purpose of capital transfer tax. In Mary Blake's case, with a net estate of £89,503.31, they came to £225 and £90 respectively, so the total probate fees to be paid were £315.

The probate fees on personal application for net estates up to £100,000 are as follows:

net estate not more than	court fee	departmental fee	total fee
£	£	£	£
1,000	NIL	2.00	2.00
2,000	NIL	5.00	5.00
5,000	NIL	5.00	5.00
6,000	NIL	6.00	6.00
7,000	NIL	7.00	7.00
8,000	NIL	8.00	8.00
9,000	NIL	9.00	9.00
10,000	NIL	10.00	10.00
25,000	40.00	(then £10.00 plus £1.00	65.00
26,000	65.00	for every additional	91.00
	(then £65 plus £2.50 for	£1,000 or part thereof)	
	every additional £1,000		
	or part thereof for		
	estates up to £100,000)		

Above £100,000 net estate, the probate court fees increase by £50 for every additional £100,000 or part of £100,000.

The probate fees must be paid when the personal representatives go to the registry to swear the papers. Payment can be made by cheque (with a supporting cheque card), banker's draft, postal order, or in cash. Matthew drew a cheque for £316.50 made payable to HM Paymaster General, on the executorship account, which he and Robert had recently opened at the bank. The extra £1.50, on top of the £315 probate fees, was for six official copies of the probate, at 25p each. Matthew had already arranged with the bank manager for the temporary overdraft.

at the probate registry

On the day appointed for their interview at the probate registry, Robert Blake and Matthew went to London, where they found Golden Cross House in Duncannon Street, near Trafalgar Square and Charing Cross station. Matthew took with him to the probate registry the file with all the papers he had accumulated in connection with Mrs Blake's estate so that he could check the accuracy of the forms they would be asked to swear as being correct. They made their way to the fifth floor, and handed in the form which they had been sent. A few minutes later they were asked to the room of the commissioner who would deal with their case.

The information which Matthew had supplied on the various probate forms had been translated on to formal printed legal documents, the executor's oath and Inland Revenue account. In the blanks were various details of the life, death and family of Mary Josephine Blake and her property. The commissioner explained that they ought to be completely satisfied that the details in the forms were true in every respect before signing. As personal representatives, theirs was the responsibility that everything was completely and accurately stated. Robert and Matthew carefully went through each part of the oath and account which seemed to tally exactly with the information which Matthew had supplied.

Satisfied that everything was in order, both Matthew and Robert signed the oath in the space provided at the end. They also signed the original will, as indicated to them by the commissioner; the oath contained a clause identifying the will as Mary Blakes's. Then, at the request of the commissioner, each of them stood up in turn, held up a copy of the New Testament in the right hand and repeated aloud these words after the commissioner: 'I swear by almighty God that this is my name and handwriting, and that the contents of this my oath are true and that this is the will referred to.' As each said the words '. . . name and handwriting' the commissioner pointed to their signatures on the oath, and likewise with the will.

Instead of swearing on the bible, a personal representative who has grounds for objecting to taking an oath can affirm by holding up his right hand and saying 'I solemnly and sincerely affirm that this . . .'

The commissioner signed beneath each of their signatures and signed the will below where they had signed it. Their business at the probate registry was now done, except for paying the probate fees. Matthew produced the cheque to the cashier, who checked it with the form and the records. Matthew also ordered six 'sealed' copies of the grant of probate, when it was issued. He reckoned that he would need this number of copies to send out, in order to avoid delays in completing the administration of the estate. These official copies are not ordinary photocopies (which anyone could take) but are copies which bear the impress of the court's seal and this is what shows them as authoritative.

letters of administration

If Mrs Blake had left no will, her next-of-kin – her children, or one of them – would have been applying for a grant of letters of administration, instead of probate; likewise, if she had left a will but it had appointed no executors, or if the executors appointed in the will did not apply for probate. In those cases, the grant would be called 'letters of administration with will annexed'.

When letters of administration are being sought, the administrators may have to provide a guarantee of their integrity. This is only likely to happen where the beneficiaries are under age or mentally disabled. The guarantee is provided by an insurance company or by individuals who undertake to make good – up to the gross value of the estate – any deficiency caused by the administrators failing in their duties. It is more likely to be required when an executor is out of the country. An insurance company will charge a fee for agreeing to act as guarantor, and will usually have the appropriate forms already drawn up.

capital transfer tax

CTT, on most assets, has to be paid before the grant of probate is issued. That is why it is often necessary to borrow money to pay the tax: in a sense it has to be paid in advance, that is, before the assets of the estate can be made available for the purpose of paying the tax.

Interest is charged on all outstanding CTT on death from the end of the sixth month after death, at 6 per cent per annum. But for houses, buildings, land, a family business and some unquoted shares it is possible to pay CTT by instalments in 8 yearly, or 16 half-yearly, payments. (The whole of the outstanding tax then becomes immediately due if the property is sold.)

It is worth considering taking up the instalments option where this is allowed. This can operate as a means of delaying the payment of most of the tax on the house until after you have got the grant of probate, so saving having to pay interest on a loan or overdraft, which is generally at a higher rate than what is charged on overdue tax.

Matthew received a form from the probate office, headed 'The estate of *Mary Josephine Blake* deceased' and informing him that in addition to the probate fees which he had already paid, he should now send a cheque for CTT, made payable to 'Inland Revenue', for £11,076.16. The assessment of CTT was the official calculation of tax on the basis of the value of the net estate, as disclosed in the forms they had completed. The net estate means the value of the assets, less the debts (including the mortgage) and the funeral expenses.

The basis of charging CTT on death is as follows. All property left to the widow or widower is exempt from capital transfer tax. The first £55,000 of the net estate is also exempt from tax; that is, on the estate not left to the widow or widower, you pay only on the excess over £55,000.

After allowing for these exemptions, the rates of CTT payable on a death are calculated in slices. At present, these are:

—on the slice £55,000 to £75,000   30 per cent
—on the slice £75,000 to £100,000   35 per cent
—on the slice £100,000 to £130,000 40 per cent
—on the slice £130,000 to £165,000 45 per cent
—on the slice £165,000 to £200,000 50 per cent
—on the slice £200,000 to £250,000 55 per cent

The rate of CTT climbs higher and higher by slices, until on an estate of more than £2.5 million, the slice above £2,500,000 is taxed at 75 per cent.

This is how the £11,076.16 for CTT was arrived at:

		£
Value of assets, including house		£91,309.31
Debts: ordinary	£227.06	
funeral	£410.50	
mortgage	£1,168.44	
		£1,806.00
	Net estate	89,503.31

CTT		£
on first £55,000		nil
on next £20,000 at 30 per cent		6,000
on remaining £14,503.31 at 35 per cent		5,076.16
		11,076.16

However Matthew elected to pay the tax on the house by 16 half-yearly instalments. The first of these would become due at the beginning of the month after 6 months had elapsed since the date of death, which is the date that interest starts to run on tax unpaid, namely 1 August 1983.

So Matthew had to pay only the tax payable on the other items in the estate. This is simply worked out as a proportion of the total. The property with the instalments option was £43,831.56 (value of house minus outstanding mortgage), so the rest of the estate was £45,671.75; the tax immediately payable was therefore: $£ \dfrac{45,671.75}{89,503.31} \times 11,076.16 = £5,651.95.$

the grant
While there may be an interval of six weeks or more between lodging the probate papers and being asked to come to the registry to sign and swear them, after that things tend to move quickly. If there is no CTT to be paid, for instance where the net estate is less than £55,000 or where all the deceased's property goes to the spouse, the grant of probate (or letters of administration) will be issued straightaway.

If CTT has to be paid, it takes two or three weeks from when the papers are signed and sworn to being told how much CTT is payable, and the grant is usually ready within a week of the CTT cheque being cleared. If there is likely to be any delay, or a technicality is holding things up, the personal representatives should be informed by the probate registry. A further visit to the registry is sometimes necessary.

In Matthew's case, there was no hitch: the grant of probate arrived by first class post, dated 14 March.

It was signed by an officer of the probate registry, and the essence of it read as follows '. . . the last Will and Testament (a copy of which is hereunto annexed) of the said deceased was proved and registered in the Principal Probate Registry of the High Court of Justice and administration of all the estate which by law devolves to and vests in the personal representative of the said deceased was granted by the aforesaid court to Matthew John Seaton and Robert Anthony Blake'.

Attached to the probate was a photocopy of the will, the original will being kept at Somerset House in London; but Matthew noticed that each page of the copy will bore the impress of the court's official seal. It was accompanied by a note which very briefly explained the procedure for collecting in the estate and advised representatives to obtain legal advice in the event of any dispute or difficulty.

The grant was what they had been striving for. It confirmed that they were entitled to deal with Mrs Blake's property, to pay her debts, and then to distribute the property in accordance with her will. It is a public document in the sense that anybody, including any beneficiary, and even the press, can obtain a copy of it or of the will from Somerset House for a small fee.

administration

When he had the probate, Matthew lost no time in proceeding with the administration. Enclosed with the probate were the six sealed copies of it for which he had asked. With these it was possible to proceed with the administration more quickly. Instead of having to send the probate in turn to each outfit requiring to see it, it was possible to send it to the bank, the insurance company, the Department for National Savings and the inspector of taxes, for instance, and two of the companies in which Mary Blake had investments, all on the same day, by sending one of the sealed copies to each of them.

Matthew wrote a similar letter to all those who had to see the probate.

> *14 Twintree Avenue*
> *Minford, Surrey*
>
> Dear Sir,
>
> Re: Mary Josephine Blake deceased
>
> I enclose a sealed copy of the probate of the will of the above for registration with you. Please return it to me when this has been done, and send me what is due to the estate as described in your letter to me of . . .
>
> Yours faithfully,
>
> *Matthew Seaton*

He sent this letter to the insurance company, the secretary of the firm's pension scheme, the Department of Health and Social Security (about the arrears of retirement pension) and the inspector of taxes (about the tax refund). He got from the post office the claim form for the National Savings bank account and certificates and the premium bonds. He completed the form and signed it in front of a witness, and sent it in the business-reply envelope which the post office had provided. Only one copy of the probate was required.

To the bank manager Matthew wrote the following letter:

14 Twintree Avenue
Minford, Surrey

15 March 1983

Dear Sir,

Re: Mary Josephine Blake deceased

I now enclose a sealed copy of the probate of the will and shall be glad if you will return it to me when you have recorded details of it. Will you please now close the deceased's current account at your branch and transfer the money in it to the executorship account which my co-executor (Robert A. Blake) and I recently opened at your branch.

I am now collecting the rest of the assets and this will result in our being able to pay off the loan account in the near future.

Yours faithfully,

Matthew Seaton

There was £193.52 in Mary Blake's current account when she died. The cheques for the CTT (£5,651.95) and the probate fees (£315) had given rise to a debit amounting to £5,966.95 on the loan account and this was now reduced by the funds from the deceased's own bank account. Banks as a rule do not allow the credit on the deceased's bank account to be treated as available for a beneficiary's use until probate is obtained. As a result a son, for instance, may be faced with paying overdraft interest to a bank while at the same time there is money available in the same bank which stands to the credit of an account which is beneficially his.

Within a few days, the £4,068.97 from the insurance company arrived; and, not long after, the Department for National Savings wrote asking for the savings certificates and the premium bond certificates, which Matthew sent. The money, including the £1,500 from the premium bonds, was received in a further week's time. No premium bond prizes had been declared in the interim. However, if an executor wants to get repayment of bonds without a grant, any prize one of the ERNIEs might have won in the meantime would have to be added to the sum, as part of the £1,500 which the Department is allowed to pay out without being shown the sealed copy of probate. (So, in Matthew's case, even the smallest prize would have made this impossible because the number of bonds which Mary Blake held were the absolute limit.)

When a copy of the probate was returned by one of the organisations which owed money to the estate, Matthew sent it off to any others who had not yet seen it. All who had to pay money to the executors required to see it, and enter details of it in their records; this is often referred to as 'registering the probate'. They usually put their stamp on the back of the probate. Soon all the money which was to be paid to the estate had been received by Matthew and paid into the executorship account at the bank. The loan, and the interest on it, was paid off, and the account stood in credit. Matthew obtained from the bank a separate note of the amount of interest because this could be deducted later on from the income in the estate. It was for £74.12.

hire purchase on the dishwasher

The next task was to deal with the hire purchase on the dishwasher. He had written to the finance company soon after his mother-in-law's death to explain that no instalments could be paid until after the grant of probate was obtained. He now decided that the easiest thing to do was to pay all the outstanding instalments in one. Rather than go through the paraphernalia of continuing the hire purchase agreement in the name of Mrs Blake's son, he sent to the finance company a cheque for what was outstanding – £46.20 – plus £1 for the actual purchase of the machine. He got a receipt, and there was no further difficulty. Sometimes a hire purchase company gives a rebate when a hire purchase debt is paid off early in this way.

He could, if he had preferred, have arranged for the agreement to be continued in Mark Blake's name, or in the name of the executors, in which case he would still have paid the instalments out of the estate.

CTT rectification

When there is no provisional agreement with the district valuer about the value of a house, the first contact with him is after probate has been obtained. Where this happens, the value of the house as finally agreed with the district valuer may be higher than the value included in the Inland

Revenue account. This results in a further payment of CTT having to be made at this stage.

Matthew heard from the district valuer for Minford who considered that Matthew's figure of £45,000 for The Firs was too low. After some bargaining, they agreed that the figure should be £46,000. Shortly after, Matthew received a further assessment from the Inland Revenue. A further £350 (for the extra £1,000 at 35 per cent) was payable. He could either send a cheque for the full amount of this, or for one sixteenth, which was the proportion for the first instalment of the option which was already due (the balance, being the proportion of the total tax attributable to the home, was payable by instalments with the rest of the instalment tax). Matthew sent to the CTT office in London a cheque for £21.88, payable to Inland Revenue.

Additional tax would also become due at this stage if the executors discovered some asset of which they had no knowledge when the papers were signed. They may, for instance, find that the deceased had a deposit account at a bank which was different from the bank where he kept his current account, or an 'ex-dividend' amount had not been ascertainable in time. Where this happens, details have to be given to the capital taxes office, and it may be necessary to sign a further, corrective, document. Occasionally, if an asset was mistakenly overestimated in value, or if a new debt appears, there may be some tax to be returned to the personal representatives.

Matthew had heard from the inspector of taxes with details of the amount of income tax repayment due to Mrs Blake's estate. He agreed this and applied to the inspector of taxes for repayment. Having obtained the figure, Matthew wrote again to the CTT office, advising them of the difference between the estimated figure he had put down on form 44 and the amount actually payable. This was the final figure still outstanding before he could apply for form 30.

Form 30 is the formal application to the CTT office for a certificate that all CTT has now been paid on the assets disclosed. However, if the executor has taken advantage of the sixteen half-yearly (or 8 annual) instalment option, the certificate will not be issued until the tax has been paid on all the outstanding instalments. Matthew could pay off all the tax because, now that he had got probate, he could deal with the shares and get the necessary money from selling some of them. Where this is not the case, for instance where the home is the only property, it could be eight years before form 30 is issued, when all tax has been paid.

selling some of the shares

Matthew knew that he had to set aside £450 to pay the legacies, later, and there was also the mortgage and other debts to pay off, as well as the rest of the CTT. So Matthew, having discussed it with Robert and Emma, decided to sell as many stocks and shares as was necessary to raise at least £7,300. He decided to sell the small holdings first (most of which happened to have gone up in value since the date of death) and so he sold the Courtaulds, Metal Box, Unilever, Parker Knoll and Norwich City Stock. He did this through the bank, sending sealed copies of the probate and the certificates for the company registrars. The bank let him have a stock transfer form for each holding, and Matthew and Robert signed them, as executors.

It is not possible to sell stocks or shares direct, without a broker. When it is done through the bank, it is the bank's broker who does the actual selling. If Matthew or Robert had been in the habit of buying and selling stocks and shares, they would have gone to one of their own brokers. Selling through a bank's broker attracts the same commission as any other broker, generally around 1.65 per cent of what the sale brings in, with a minimum fee of £10 per holding which is charged if the 1.65 per cent comes to less than that amount. The bank may also charge a dealing fee.

The formalities for selling and transferring government (so called gilt-edged) stock are very similar to ordinary stock and shares, but the registrar is the Bank of England in the City of London.

The sales of Mary Blake's shares raised a total of £7,543.16 after deduction of commission and fees. The money was sent to Matthew ten days later, and he paid it in to the executorship account.

He made a note of the prices at which the shares were sold, to compare with the value at the date of Mrs Blake's death, in case there should be liability for capital gains tax.

form 30

Matthew received, and completed, two copies of form 30. One copy would eventually be returned to him with the certificate on the second page signed and stamped, as an acknowledgement that the capital taxes office is satisfied, on the basis of the information disclosed, that no further CTT was due. If any further tax is due, the certificate is only sent when this is paid.

Form 30 was simple to complete. The applicants were the two executors; Mrs Blake's name and date of death had to be stated and that the 'occasion of liability' was under the will of Mrs Mary Josephine Blake. For assets, in section D, Matthew wrote 'as disclosed in form 44, and increase in value of house as shown on CTT assessment form dated 6 April 1983.' There was one further addition or amendment about which he had to give information. He wrote 'adjustment of income tax repayments due to the estate (previous estimate £150, actual repayment £193.15).' CTT was payable at 35% on the increased amount of the income tax repayment so he calculated the tax at 35% on £43.15 (namely £15.10) and drew a cheque for the total CTT still payable, including this amount, which came to £5,767.43 and would clear all the instalments of CTT on the house, too.

In section E he wrote that the beneficiaries were 'legatees under the will'. If there had not been a will, the entry should have read 'persons entitled under the intestacy of' and the name of the deceased person.

There were no other material facts, so Matthew and Robert signed both copies of form 30 and sent them to The Capital Taxes Office, Rockley Road, London W14 0DF, with the cheque.

Although it says on form 30 that it should not be submitted until the applicant has reason to believe that no adjustment to the amount of capital transfer tax paid will be necessary, if an asset or a debt should, after all, be disclosed later, the matter can be reopened.

It is only when the second copy of form 30, with the certificate signed and stamped, is returned, that the personal representatives can safely proceed to distribute the money they have in hand to those entitled to it, secure in the knowledge that the capital taxes office will not later be claiming more tax.

The form 30 has the effect of fixing the value of assets conclusively as at the date of death. If a sale of, for example, a house is expected to raise a much larger figure than that disclosed or agreed with the district valuer, it may be an indication that a higher valuation should have been put on the particular asset concerned. So it may be prudent, in such a case, to wait until form 30 is obtained before going ahead with the sale, because until form 30 is obtained the question of value can be re-opened.

paying off debts
Matthew could now pay the debts; the gas bill, the telephone account, garage, and wines and spirits bills. He also paid the funeral bill.

transferring the shares

The next item to be dealt with was the remaining shares Mrs Blake had owned, investments of a kind which, in normal times, Matthew might well have chosen, if asked to advise on the subject. He suggested that the two children who were entitled to the residue of the estate should divide and should take over, as they stood, the unsold investments which their mother had held; and they agreed.

It is often necessary to sell some or all of the shares held by a person who has died, in order to pay the debts, CTT or the legacies or to meet the expenses of administering the estate. Where this happens, as in Matthew's case, it is then the remaining shares which get divided according to the will.

Where shares or unit trust holdings are sold within a year of a death, for less than the value on the date of death, the total of the gross selling price of all such investments sold within the year can be substituted for the value for CTT. The sale has to be made by the executors; once the shares have been transferred into the names of the beneficiaries it is too late to claim a reduction of CTT. Adjustment is made by a corrective document.

Whether the shares are sold or not, it is necessary for each company in which shares are held to see a copy of the probate. A letter addressed to the registrar of the company at the head office will always ultimately reach the right destination.

In a case where a sole executor is also the person entitled to the shares under the will, no formal transfer of the shares is usually needed. Instead a document called a letter of request (form CON41A published by Oyez Stationery) can be used and this is not liable to any stamp duty.

Where the shares are to be sold, or where (as in Mrs Blake's case) the shares are to be transferred direct to the beneficiaries (the people entitled to have them under the will), it is usually possible to send the probate to the registrar of the company at the same time as sending the transfer of the shares to be dealt with by him.

The unsold shares comprised part of the residue of the estate – not having been left to anyone else. This meant that, under the will, Mrs Blake's two children, Emma and Robert, were entitled to the shares equally. It would therefore be necessary to value shares again because their relative worth would have changed since the date of death and Emma and Robert were entitled to equal value as at the date the administration was ended. Administration ends when all debts are paid and all the taxes dealt with including those for the period of administration. If the beneficiaries do not split the actual holdings, a valuation is needed as at the date of completion of administration, and the administration or estate account should show this.

It is perfectly possible to divide up each existing holding of shares. One way – perhaps the fairest if there is any prospect of disagreements or resentment – is to divide each holding among the beneficiaries. Then each one gets exactly the same. This is what Robert and Emma, on Matthew's advice, decided to do.

Alternatively, the beneficiaries can agree in writing who is to take over what shares on what day, using the stock exchange closing prices as shown in the financial columns of the national press. Fine adjustments, needed to achieve exact divisions, can be made out of any cash balance in hand. If no agreement is possible, all the shares should be sold and the beneficiaries then get their entitlement in cash. Then there can be no argument about who gets what, but from an investment point of view this may not be the most advantageous thing to do.

A bank is an obvious choice for the job of attending to the stamping of the transfers as part of the operation of sending them to the companies concerned. Matthew therefore took the stock and shares certificates, together with the copies of the probate, to the Minford branch of Barminster Bank, and asked the manager to deal with them. Where executors employ the bank to lodge the transfers for registration, they may as well let the bank do the whole thing, merely sending the stock certificates to the bank manager with appropriate detailed instructions (about who is to get what) for the necessary action.

The bank would debit the executorship account with the stamp duty of 50p per transfer, and the company registrars' fees, and the bank's own fee.

Some banks do not charge, treating it as a courtesy service to their customers, others charge between £2 and £5 per transfer, but this fee includes the service of providing and completing the transfer forms.

It is also possible to obtain stock transfer forms from an Oyez shop, complete them for each of the stocks held and send them to the companies concerned so that the beneficiaries can be registered as the new owners. The form is called CON 40, and on the back of it is a list of transactions in regard of which a flat fee of 50p per transfer is payable (instead of *ad valorem*, that is a percentage of the value, stamp duty). Category (e) of this would apply in a case of transferring stock or shares to a residuary legatee, under a will. The completed forms should be sent with a cheque for the total amount (50 pence per form) to the Controller of Stamps, Direct Post

Section, West Block, Barrington Road, Worthing, Sussex, who will return them stamped.

The transfer forms, stock or share certificates, and a copy of the grant of probate have then to be sent to the registrars of the companies concerned.

Eventually Matthew received back the sealed copies of the probate together with the new stock and share certificates showing Mrs Blake's two elder children as the owners of their new holding of shares. This was proof of ownership of the shares.

capital gains tax

Matthew had to consider the capital gains tax position. This is payable when assets are sold for a higher price than they cost when they were bought or higher than their probate value, that is their valuation at the time of the owner's death. (For assets held for more than a year the cost, or base value, can be raised in line with the rise in the retail prices index, and so any gain may be reduced.)

If when shares are to be transferred to the beneficiaries they are showing a gain since the date of death, it could be better to sell the shares within the estate, give cash to the beneficiaries and for the beneficiaries then to buy back the shares with the cash. The shares will then obtain a higher base value for any future sale. However, the beneficiaries will need to hold them for a year before they can obtain the benefit of the indexation of base value.

Every person is allowed £5000 of gains in each tax year (from 6 April to the following 5th April) without paying any tax (and any losses can be offset against any gains). The executors of an estate have their own £5,000 exemption each year, independently of the beneficiaries who are entitled to the assets. This offers considerable scope for avoiding or lessening gains, and utilising losses, to be offset against gains. The £5,000 exemption for executors is available for the tax year in which the deceased died, and for each of the two following years. If, therefore, the beneficiaries are likely to have their own gains for any of these years, it may be better for the executor to continue to hold the shares in the administration of the estate in case they need to be sold at a gain, which would be taxable if the beneficiaries had owned the shares, but for which the executors can use part of the £5,000 exemption.

A special rule applies to Treasury or Exchequer stock and similar so-called gilts. If the executor sells and the deceased had held the stock for at least one year, it falls outside capital gains tax considerations. Similarly if the beneficiary sells after having held the stock for at least one year, any gain in value does not have to be included in capital gains tax calculations.

In Matthew's case the shares which had been sold had all shown slight gains, but the total gain was well within the £5,000 exemption. Some of those which were transferred to Robert and Emma were showing losses. If the beneficiaries had had taxable gains in that tax year against which these losses could have been offset, the executors could have sold the shares in Robert's and Emma's names and offset the losses. However, there were none, so Robert and Emma took over the higher base value at the date of Mary Blake's death.

Where the gains are likely to be more than £5,000, it may be thought prudent to take professional advice as to how to minimise capital gains tax payable. The sale could, in such a case, perhaps be split between the executors and the beneficiaries in such a way that there would be more than one £5,000 exemption available for any one tax year. Matthew here just had to make a record of those sold within the administration for the purposes of the income tax return which he would need to fill in.

stop press

In the budget speech on 15 March 1983, the Chancellor announced an increase from £5,000 to £5,300 in the amount of gains exempt from capital gains tax.

Regarding payment of capital transfer tax on certain property (for example, houses and land) in 8 annual or 16 half-yearly instalments, he announced that in future the number of instalments will be increased to 10 but the option to pay in half-yearly instalments will no longer be available.

transfer of the house

Next, the house had to be transferred to Mark Blake and the mortgage paid off. So Matthew wrote to the building society:

14 Twintree Avenue
Minford, Surrey

5 April 1983

To: The Manager
Minford Building Society
Great Winchester Street
Minford, Surrey

Dear Sir,

Re: Mary Josephine Blake deceased, The Firs, Willow Lane, Minford

I enclose a sealed copy of the probate for registration; please return it.

The executors now wish to pay off the mortgage with your society as soon as this can be arranged, so please take this letter as formal notice to you of their intention to do this.

Please let me know how much is required to redeem the mortgage as at 25 April. I shall then arrange to let you have a cheque for that amount on that day. You will then, no doubt, forward the deeds of the house to me, together with the official receipt of the society acknowledging that the mortgage has been paid off.

On the question of insurance, we wish to continue the existing policy, but to have it transferred to the name of Mr Mark Douglas Blake (to whom the property has been bequeathed), and to take the opportunity of increasing the cover to the present value of the house, £46,000. Will you please arrange this, or put me in touch with the insurance company so that I can do so.

Yours faithfully,

Matthew Seaton

Where a mortgage is outstanding at the time of death and there is nothing in the will about having it paid off out of the residue, the house may have to be sold so that the mortgage can be paid off out of the proceeds of the sale and the beneficiary would get the balance of the money. (But many people nowadays have a mortgage protection policy or a mortgage on an endowment policy basis, so that the mortgage can be repaid automatically on the death of the borrower.) Where the house is going to be transferred outright into the name of a beneficiary, the building society may be prepared to let the beneficiary continue with the existing mortgage, or would probably grant a new mortgage. He can, of course, apply to any source – another building society, for example, or bank – for a loan.

if it is a registered property
The title to the house was a registered one. It was not strictly accurate, therefore, of Matthew to have spoken of the deeds of the house, although it is common practice even in the legal profession to do so. He really meant the charge certificate, which the building society held as part of its security for the money it had lent. When a house has a registered title, and a mortgage on it is completely paid off, the building society hands back the charge certificate to the owner, together with an official acknowledgment that the money due under the mortgage has been paid. This acknowledgment is usually on a special Land Registry form, known as form 53Co. The owner then sends the charge certificate, together with form 53Co, to the Land Registry. Some time later he receives from the registry the land certificate, which is substantially the same as the charge certificate, but with the important difference of having had the details of the mortgage officially crossed out. In this way the owner obtains formal proof of his ownership, free from any mention of a mortgage. This can take six to eight weeks or even longer, for a straightforward case.

Mrs Blake was currently registered at the Land Registry as being the owner – or registered proprietor, to use the official expression – of The Firs, Willow Lane, Minford. To prove that the executors now replaced her, the probate would have to be registered with the Land Registry. And there was a further step involved: to transfer the house into Mark Blake's name.

All three transactions could be dealt with in a single application to the Land Registry: crossing off the details of the mortgage, substituting the names of the executors for Mrs Blake's and substituting Mark Blake for the executors.

Matthew heard from the building society within a few days, and they told

him how much was required to pay off the mortgage, including a small fee
they charged. The Minford Building Society needed £1,185.31 to clear the
mortgage. Matthew sent a cheque for this amount to the building society.
A week later he received the 'deeds' by registered post: the charge
certificate, form 53Co bearing the seal of the building society, and a
number of old papers relating to the property.

Matthew next prepared the form to transfer the ownership of the house
into Mark Blake's name. He obtained from the Oyez shop a copy of Land
Registry form 56 (Assent or Appropriation). He could also have obtained
this form from HMSO, the Stationery Office.

The document by which personal representatives transfer a house to the
person entitled to it under a will or intestacy is usually called an assent
(accent on the first syllable), and they are said to assent (accent on the
second syllable) to the property vesting in the person entitled to it. Form 56
was not difficult to complete. This is how it read when Matthew had filled
in the blanks.

Form 56
HM Land Registry

ASSENT OR APPROPRIATION

County and district
(or London borough)   *Surrey*
Title number   *SY2121212*
Property   *'The Firs', Willow Lane, Minford*

(We) *Robert Anthony Blake of Wringapeak Farm, Woody Bay, North
Devon, farmer, and Matthew John Seaton of 14 Twintree Avenue,
Minford, Surrey, education officer*
                as personal representative(s) of the late *Mary Josephine
Blake of 'The Firs', Willow Lane, Minford, Surrey, widow*
hereby assent to the land comprised in the title above mentioned vesting
in: *Mark Douglas Blake*
                        of 'The Firs', Willow Lane,
                        Minford, Surrey
                        musician
Dated the   *13*   day of   *May   1983*
Signed by the said   *Robert*⎤
                                    ⎬ *Robert A. Blake*
          Anthony Blake⎦
in the presence of
Name: *Judy Gurney*
Address: *The Platt, Amersham, Bucks*
Ocupation: *political researcher*
Signed by the said   *Matthew*⎤
                                      ⎬ *M. J. Seaton*
          John Seaton⎦
in the presence of
Name: *Judy Gurney*
          as above

Form 56 can also be used for a leasehold house, in which case the landlord has to be notified. Depending on the terms of the lease, he may be entitled to receive a copy of the completed form, and to demand a fee.

When form 56 had been completed, signed by Robert Blake and Matthew, and witnessed, Matthew sent it to the appropriate district office of the Land Registry, with a covering letter:

> *14 Twintree Avenue*
> *Minford, Surrey*
>
> 13 May 1983
>
> Dear Sir,
>
> Re: 'The Firs, Willow Lane, Minford, Surrey SY2121212
>
> I enclose a sealed copy of the probate of Mary Josephine Blake's will, charge certificate for the 'The Firs', Willow Lane, forms 53Co and 56 and cheque payable to HM Land Registry for £23. Please cancel the mortgage and register Mark Douglas Blake as the new owner.
>
> Please then return the copy of the probate and the land certificate to him.
>
> Yours faithfully,
>
> *Matthew Seaton*

The £23 fee was for registering the assent to Mark Blake, based on the value of the house (there was no fee to pay for cancelling the mortgage). The back of form 56 had to be completed by stating the registered title number of the house and its value. This was needed to fix the fee to be paid for registering the transfer of the house to Mark. The fee was 50p for every £1,000 of the value of the house (with a maximum fee of £50). Matthew completed the 'Statement of Value' and crossed out the reference in the printed part of the form to other titles and values and to solicitors. Mark then signed the form in his capacity of devisee, as the form called him, that is to say the person to whom the property was devised or given by the will. He certified the value of the house as being £46,000, the figure agreed for CTT purposes, so £23 was payable.

They had an acknowledgment from the Land Registry which said how long it would take to deal with the application. Five weeks later Mark received the land certificate in which he appeared as the registered proprietor. The reference to the mortgage to the Minford Building Society had been crossed out. But there was a note in the land certificate that the property might be liable for more CTT. This was a routine formality and inapt for a case where the CTT had been paid in full and a clearance certificate issued. At the same time, the Land Registry returned the copy of the probate. Thus Mark Blake become registered as the owner of the house in substitution for his late mother, and the mortgage was cleared.

This is the procedure which must be followed irrespective of whether the ultimate owner of the property, under the will, is a beneficiary or the executor (or administrator). Even if the property is left wholly to an only executor, form 56 still needs to be completed, to transfer ownership of the property from the executor in that capacity, to himself as owner absolutely.

unregistered property
If the title to a house is not registered at the Land Registry, the procedure for transferring the house to the person entitled to it is likely to be less straightforward. To find out whether the title is registered or not, it is necessary to inspect the deeds. If there is no land certificate with the deeds, it means that the title is not registered. In a considerable number of areas, particularly towns and cities, registration of title has become compulsory, which means that the titles to properties there have had to be registered, but only when they are sold. The result is that even in areas of compulsory registration, many houses still have unregistered titles. It is not necessary (or possible) to register a title when a house changes hands on a death – only on a sale.

In the case of an unregistered title, the executor, after paying off the mortgage, if there is one, should find amongst the deeds one deed which is the conveyance of the property to the deceased when he bought it. (If the house is leasehold, it is called an assignment.) This is the deed prepared at the time the house was bought and which transferred ownership of it to the deceased. This deed should be used as the basis for preparing the document to transfer ownership to the person now entitled to it under the will or intestacy. This document is called an assent, the same name as is used in the case of a house with a registered title, and in a simple case can be prepared by the executor himself.

Imagine that Mrs Blake's house had had an unregistered title, and that the executors had wished to put the house into Mark Blake's name, now that he was entitled to it. When he had paid off the building society mortgage, Matthew would have received from the building society the title deeds to the house. These would have included the mortgage deed, at the back of which would now appear a receipt, bearing the official seal of the building society, which acknowledged that all the money due under the mortgage had now been paid off. The title deeds would also have included the deed of conveyance prepared when the house last changed hands on a purchase. Matthew would also have needed the original grant of probate. The assent, on an ordinary sheet of paper, would have read like this:

ASSENT

We hereby assent to the freehold property The Firs, Willow Lane, Minford, Surrey vesting in Mark Douglas Blake of The Firs, Willow Lane, Minford.
We make this assent as executors of the will of Mrs Mary Josephine Blake who died on 5 January 1983.
Probate of her will was granted to us by the Principal Probate Registry on 14 March 1983.
We hereby acknowledge Mark Douglas Blake's right to the production of the probate.
Dated 13 May 1983.
Signed by the executors of the will of Mary Josephine Blake deceased: Robert Anthony Blake of Wringapeak Farm, Woody Bay, North Devon, farmer, and Matthew John Seaton of 14 Twintree Avenue, Minford, education officer.
Signatures: Robert A. Blake   M. J. Seaton
Witness: Judy Gurney, The Platt, Amersham.

In many cases an assent in that form is sufficient. It should not be used where a mortgage has not yet been paid off, or where there is any complication. In the case of a joint ownership as joint tenants, as a rule, no assent is needed; a death certificate is sufficient to prove the survivor's title. The form of assent must still be used even where the beneficiary is the only (or one of several) personal representative, writing what in effect is an assent to himself.

If this form of assent is used for a leasehold house, details of the lease should appear in the assent and the landlord should be notified; he may be entitled to a copy of the assent itself and he may demand a fee, depending on the terms of the lease.

An assent is not liable for stamp duty, and does not have to be registered anywhere. It has to be put with the deeds, and there it stays.

registered or unregistered

One formality remains, however, whether the title is registered or not. There should be written or typed on the back of the original grant of probate a brief memorandum giving the essential details of the assent. In the case of Mrs Blake's house, it would have to say something like this:

Memo: An assent dated 13 May 1983 vested the freehold house The Firs, Willow Lane, Minford, Surrey in Mark Douglas Blake, and his right to the production of this grant of probate was acknowledged.

Mark Blake, as beneficiary, is given a specific legal right to be shown at any time the original grant of probate, as he may need to when he comes to sell the house, in which case the grant of probate is one of the documents needed to prove his ownership. In this way, anyone who buys the property from Mark is given legal protection, especially against fraud.

A difficulty in preparing an assent in the case of unregistered property lies in the fact that there is no one to check it unless and until the property comes to be sold, when the buyer's solicitor will want to look at it. If the executors die before the house comes to be sold and it turns out that the assent was incorrect in some respect, there might be considerable expense and difficulty in putting things right. In the case of registered property, however, the beneficiary knows that the assent is correct as soon as the land certificate, showing him as the new owner, is received back from the Land Registry.

distribution according to the will

Little remained for Matthew to do to complete the administration. Having made sure that all expenses and all debts had been paid, he was in a position to make a final distribution.

All the expenses involved in the administration of the estate had been paid out of the executorship account at the bank. These expenses included the cost of copies of the probate, the stamp duty and bank's charge on the transfer of shares and the Land Registry fees relating to the transfer of the house. His own out-of-pocket expenses, on postage and such matters as fares to London to visit the probate registry, were refunded out of the executorship account, and so were Robert Blake's expenses as an executor. Personal representatives are not entitled to be paid for the time they devote to the administration of the estate, unless the will specifically says so. But, on the other hand, they are not expected to dip into their own pockets.

the personal effects

The will left 'furniture and effects' in the house to Mark. He took them over with the house itself, including the three paintings, and they became his property without any formalities. Matthew asked him to write a letter addressed to the executors, confirming that the furniture and effects and car were now in his possession as owner, and were no longer part of the estate. A car may or may not be covered by the expression personal effects; normally it would be, but it is much better, in a will, to make clear the testator's intention by dealing with a car specifically, as Mrs Blake had done.

receipts

The executors were now in a position to pay the legacies and distribute amongst the beneficiaries the specific requests. Robert and Matthew signed the cheques on the executorship account for the pecuniary legacies which Mrs Blake had given in her will. They obtained a receipt from each of the beneficiaries. Mrs Ward's read as follows:

Mary Josephine Blake deceased
I acknowledge that I have received the sum of one hundred pounds (£100) from Matthew J. Seaton and Robert A. Blake in settlement of the legacy due to me under the will of my late friend, Mary J. Blake.

Dated: 9 June 1983.
Signed: Angela Ward (Mrs).

The will had also provided that Josef Samson should receive the carriage clock which had belonged to Mary Blake. Matthew wrote to him telling him about this and when Mr Samson came to collect the clock, obtained from him this acknowledgment:

Mary Josephine Blake deceased
I acknowledge that I have received the carriage clock left to me by the will of the late Mrs Mary Blake.

Dated: 12 June 1983.
Signed: Josef R. Samson.

children under 18
As far as the £50 legacies to each of the grandchildren were concerned, there was no problem about any over 18 years old. So far as those under 18 were concerned, there arose the legal difficulty that money or property cannot validly be handed over to a minor – even a seventeen-year-old. The £50 could not be paid to the grandchildren directly because a person under eighteen does not have the legal capacity to give the executors a receipt. So there is always the risk of the minor, who received his money before being of age, coming along and demanding his money again after his eighteenth birthday. The executors. therefore, had to invest the money until each child, on becoming eighteen, could receive his or her share (plus the interest it had earned meanwhile).

Matthew and Robert opened a National Savings Bank investment account in their own names for the two grandchildren under 18. The alternative was a building society account, but this tends to give a very low rate of return where the account holders do not pay any income tax. Although income tax is deemed to have been deducted at source, you are not allowed to reclaim it from the Inland Revenue. So the National Savings bank investment account, Matthew thought, would give the grandchildren more income.

It would be possible for the executors to pay out the interest for the children's benefit, but Matthew and Robert thought that it would be better for it to accrue in the account until they each became of age.

Where an administration is long and complicated, it is possible that the legacies could not be paid for several years. When the legacy is actually paid the legatee (the one receiving the legacy), is entitled not only to the actual amount of the legacy but also to interest at 5 per cent per annum from the date one year after the date of death until payment of the legacy.

the residue

Matthew was about to take the conclusive step in the administration, the final distribution of the residue. Personal representatives should consider carefully everything they have done before parting with the remaining asset.

final tax matters

If any income (such as dividends, or interest on a deposit account) has been received between the date of death and the proposed date of distribution of the assets, it is necessary to obtain an income tax form (R59) which is a statement of trust income received, so that any liability to tax on that income which might arise can be discharged.

He could not finally distribute the residue until he knew that all the income tax and capital gains tax was finalised. He had received the 'xd' dividend on the Stonehill shares, and there were also some others which had just come in. He completed a return, showing all these, and also told the Inland Revenue that the gain on the shares sold was less than £5,000. He set out the calculation to prove this.

There was no tax to pay because the interest on the post office account was less than £70 and all the other income had already had the tax paid at the basic rate before he received it. In fact, Matthew was due for a small repayment of income tax because he could also offset the £74.12 interest paid on the loan account; he received shortly a repayment of £22.24. Had there been nothing to offset against the dividends, no repayment would have been due because an estate is taxed on all the income at 30 per cent: no personal allowances are available.

the last steps

Matthew went through everything that he had done in connection with the executorship from the moment his mother-in-law had died nearly six months before. He looked again at every asset in the estate, he looked at each debt, and at each expense, to see that everything had been done properly. This is important if several people are sharing the residue, and it would have been more important still if there had been any dissent within the family. Reviewing all his actions over the previous months, Matthew found everything to be in order. Thus the executors were in a position to make the final distribution by dividing into two the balance standing to the credit of the executorship bank account. This cleared the executorship bank account, which they then closed.

Matthew went through the details of the administration with Robert, showing him exactly what had been done. He prepared, and they both signed, accounts showing what everyone had received and how it was arrived at, taking into account all the receipts and payments that had been through their hands. It was not necessary that these accounts should take any particular form. They merely showed a list of the assets, distinguished between those which had been taken over in kind (the house, the contents of the house, the car, the clock, the jewellery and the shares), and those which had been sold or converted into money. They showed the value of all the assets at the date of death, and thus could then be referred to on any future sales by Robert and Emma for capital gains tax purposes.

They showed the debts, the funeral expenses, and the administration expenses, and then showed the balance in hand. The legacies were set out in the account and the net balance was the amount which was shared equally between Emma and Robert. Each of them kept a signed copy of the accounts.

In this way, the administration by the executors was brought to an end. Matthew bundled all the papers together, including the original probate and the signed copy of the account, and put them in a large envelope to be kept in a safe place, theoretically for twelve years. The administration of the estate was over.

distribution on intestacy

The procedure adopted by personal representatives is broadly the same whether they are executors (appointed in a will) who apply for a grant of probate, or administrators (on an intestacy) who apply for a grant of letters of administration. But when it comes to distributing the estate, the executors follow the wishes of the deceased according to the will. Administrators must apply the intestacy rules laid down in the Administration of Estates Act.

The nearest next-of-kin are entitled to apply for the grant. If the nearest relation does not wish to apply, he can renounce his right to do so, in which case the next-nearest becomes entitled to be the administrator, and so on, down the line of kinship. The widow, or widower, is primarily entitled to be the administrator.

If there is no surviving spouse, or if he or she does not apply for a grant, then any of the children may apply. Grandchildren may apply, if their parents are dead. Next, the deceased's parents may apply, and then brothers and sisters, or their children. They are followed by half-brothers and half-sisters, or their children. Next grandparents, followed by uncles and aunts (or their children) may apply, finishing up with uncles and aunts of the half blood, or their children. No relations remoter than those are legally next-of-kin so as to be entitled to apply for a grant of letters of administration. Normally it is not necessary to have more than one administrator, but where someone under 18 is entitled to the estate, or part of it, or where a life interest arises under the intestacy rules, there must be at least two administrators.

The division of the net estate where a person died without leaving a will depends on the value of what is left, and what family survives. The net estate is what remains of the estate after paying the debts, the funeral expenses, the CTT, the expenses of getting the letters of administration, and of administering the estate. Here are some examples.

where the deceased left a wife or husband

example a

deceased's family
Wife and three children.

net estate
Personal effects (that is, strictly, 'personal chattels', including car – unless it was used for business purposes – furniture, clothing, jewellery and all goods and chattels) and £9,500 (in savings bank, savings certificates, house).

division of estate under intestacy rules
All to wife.

explanation
The surviving spouse takes the personal effects, no matter how great their value, and the first £40,000 of the rest. In the present example this is less than £40,000, so everything goes to the surviving spouse, and the children get nothing. No other relatives (for example, parents) are entitled to any part of the estate. It would be the same in the case of a wife dying intestate.

---

example b

deceased's family
Wife and four children.

net estate
Personal effects and £44,000 including investments and value of house.

division of estate under intestacy rules
(1) wife gets:
  (a) personal effects
  (b) £40,000 plus interest on it at 7 per cent per annum from date of death (not, as for a pecuniary legacy under a will, one year from the date of death) until payment
  (c) a life interest in £2,000 (that is, the income from £2,000 for the rest of her life)
(2) each of four children gets:
  (a) £500 immediately
  (b) £500 on their mother's death.

explanation
The intestacy rules give the widow all the personal effects, £40,000 (plus interest at 7 per cent from the date of death to the date of payment) and a life interest in half the remainder. The children share the second half of the remainder immediately, and the first half on their mother's death. If one of the children had died before the father, leaving any children, then those grandchildren of the deceased would have shared their parent's proportion

of their grandfather's estate. It makes no difference if the widow is not the mother of some or all of the children; where, for instance, their father married a second time, the estate is shared as decribed between the widow and the deceased's children, both her children by him and her stepchildren. Any children or grandchildren under age do not inherit unless and until coming of age or getting married. Other relatives (parents, or stepchildren, of the deceased, for instance) get nothing.

---

example c

deceased's family
Husband, mother, no children.

net estate
Personal effects, £32,000 in investments.

division of estate under intestacy rules
All to husband.

explanation
Where there are no children, the surviving husband or wife takes all the personal effects, plus everything else up to £85,000. Mother gets nothing.

---

example d

deceased's family
Wife, mother and father, two brothers, no children.

net estate
Personal effects, £95,000 in investments and house.

division of estate under intestacy rules
(1) wife gets:
  (a) personal effects
  (b) £85,000, plus interest on it at 7 per cent per annum from date of death until payment
  (c) £5,000
(2) mother gets £2,500
(3) father gets £2,500

explanation
The surviving wife or husband takes the personal effects and £85,000, plus interest until payment. The rest is divided in two; the surviving spouse takes one half, and the other half is divided equally between the deceased's parents (the brothers get nothing). If there had been only one parent alive, he or she would have received the whole of the parents' £5,000. If he had no parents living, his brothers would share equally that £5,000; the share of any brother or sister who died before the deceased would be divided equally between his or her children.

---

example e

deceased's family
Husband, no children, no parents, no brothers or sisters, no nephews or nieces, no grandparents; one aunt, four cousins.

new estate
Personal effects, £140,000 in investments

division of estate under intestacy rules
All to husband

explanation
If, apart from the surviving spouse, the nearest relations are aunts, uncles, cousins, or grandparents (that is, no children, parents or siblings, nephews or nieces), the surviving spouse takes everything, no matter how much it is.

where the deceased left no wife or husband

example f

deceased's family
No wife, three children, seven grandchildren, two of whom are children of
a son who died some years before.

net estate
£3,500, personal effects to the value of £500; total £4,000.

division of estate under intestacy rules
(1) each of the three surviving children gets £1,000 ($\times$ 3 = £3,000)
(2) each of the two grandchildren whose father died before the deceased
     gets £500 ($\times$ 2 = £1,000)
(3) the other grandchildren get nothing.

explanation
Where there is no wife or husband, the whole estate is shared between the
children equally. It makes no difference how big or small the estate is. The
share of any child who has already died is shared equally between his
children; this process of taking a deceased parent's share can go on to the
third and fourth generation, if necessary. Any children or grandchildren
who are under age do not get a share until they come of age, or marry.

---

example g

deceased's family
Two brothers.

net estate
£3,000 including personal effects.

division of estate under intestacy rules
1,500 to each brother.

explanation
If the parents of a bachelor or a spinster (or widow or widower without descendants) are both dead, the whole estate is shared between brothers and sisters equally. The share of a deceased brother or sister goes to his or her children. If there had been a parent alive, he or she would have taken everything, and brothers and sisters would have received nothing. If both parents are alive, they share the estate equally.

Relatives of the whole blood take priority over relatives of the half blood. If, for example, a bachelor whose parents are dead has one brother and one half-brother, the brother takes everything and the half-brother takes nothing. But if there is no brother of the whole blood, then a half-brother would take everything in priority to grandparents, or aunts, uncles or cousins. The same applies to other relatives of the half blood: they only take if corresponding relatives of the whole blood (or their descendants) are not alive to inherit a share. An illegitimate child or an adopted child counts as being a child of the full blood for the purpose of inheritance.

---

example h

deceased's family
One aunt, two uncles, three cousins who are children of one deceased uncle, four cousins who are children of one deceased aunt, five cousins who are children of the two living uncles; no children, no parents, no brothers or sisters, no grandparents.

net estate
£6,000.

division of estate under intestacy rules
(1) £1,200 each to the aunt and two uncles ($\times 3 = £3,600$)
(2) £400 each to the three cousins who are children of the deceased uncle ($\times 3 = £1,200$)
(3) £300 each to the four cousins who are children of the deceased aunt ($\times 4 = £1,200$).

explanation
The aunts and uncles, being the nearest relatives, share the estate equally. But the children of any dead aunt or dead uncle share what the aunt or uncle would have received if he or she had survived long enough. So the estate is divided into five; the one-fifth share of the dead uncle is divided into three equal shares for his children (the three cousins on that side of the family), and the one-fifth share of the dead aunt is divided into four equal shares for the children (the four cousins on that side of the family). The cousins whose relevant parent is still alive get nothing.

---

example j

deceased's family
Five second cousins (relatives who have the same great-grandparents as the deceased).

net estate
£10,000.

division of estate under intestacy rules
Everything to the crown.

explanation
Only relatives who can show that they are descendants of (or are) the deceased's grandparents can take a share in the estate of someone who died intestate. To be a descendant of the deceased's great-grandparent is not sufficient, and if there are no nearer relatives, the estate goes to the crown. It is then called *bona vacantia*, property to which no one can claim a title. Often the Treasury Solicitor, who administers *bona vacantia*, makes a distribution of some or even all of the net estate, after paying the expenses, among those who can show a strong moral claim: where a distant relative has looked after the deceased for many years, for example, or where a void will has been made which would have left everything to a close friend. This may also happen where the deceased had been living with a woman to whom he was not married. But she is likely to do better by claiming under the Inheritance (Provision for Family and Dependants) Act 1975, since she would count as being someone who 'immediately before the death of the

deceased was being maintained either wholly or partly by the deceased'. This would give her a right to claim reasonable provision – probably an income, but perhaps a capital sum as well – out of the estate. Such a claim should be made without delay. The procedure for this is complicated enough to warrant seeking legal advice.

who inherits the property of a bachelor who died intestate

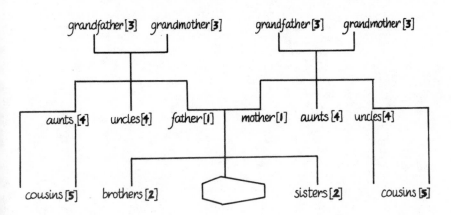

index

What to do when someone dies

This book is a companion volume to *Wills and probate*. It aims to help those who have never had to deal with the arrangements that must be made after a death – getting a doctor's certificate and registering the death, deciding whether to bury or cremate, choosing an undertaker and a coffin, putting notices in the papers, selecting the form of service, claiming national insurance benefits. It explains the function of people with whom they will come in contact, often for the first time. They will get help and guidance from the doctor, the registrar, the undertaker, the clergyman, the cemetery or crematorium officials, the Department of Health and Social Security and, in some circumstances, the police and the coroner. However, it is the executor or nearest relative who has to make the decisions, often at a time of personal distress. The book describes what needs to be done, when, and how to set about it.

No attempt is made to deal with the personal or social aspects of death, such as the psychology of grief and shock, the rituals and conventions of mounning, or attitudes to death.

Earning money at home

for anyone who wants or needs to take up an activity at home that will bring some extra (or essential) cash, this book sets out what is entailed. It puts forward the pros and cons of working at home, stressing the self-discipline required and the reorganisation that may be necessary. The statutory requirements about planning permission, liability for insurance, national insurance and tax are all explained. Advertising and getting work, costing and charging for it, getting supplies, keeping accounts, are all important factors that are fully covered. The second section of the book suggests some types of work that might be suitable, with or without previous experience, giving a brief account of what may be involved in undertaking them. Courses for brushing up a skill or hobby to a more professional standard are suggested, and sources of further help and advice are given. The final section discusses what to do if your venture fares badly and, more optimistically, how to expand the business when successful.

Starting your own business

looks at the stages involved in setting up and running your own business, from the initial idea to locating the market, finding premises, using promotion techniques, meeting demands. It deals with finance, explaining the difference between start-up and working capital, and gives meaning to such terms as overheads, materials costs, pricing, profit and loss forecasting, setting up a cash-flow forecast. It deals with tax and explains how business income tax is assessed, why voluntary registration for VAT could be advantageous. Even without a financial background, you will find the 'money' sections easy to understand.

The book highlights the respective advantages and disadvantages of being a sole trader, a partnership or a limited company; alternatives such as co-operatives and franchising are also discussed. One section is devoted to exporting and makes this intricate subject easy for anyone to follow. Throughout the book, sources of advice are indicated, including the government and private organisations' help for new business.

Getting a new job

is a practical guide to the steps to take from when one job ends to the day the next one begins. The circumstances relating to unfair dismissal are explained and the remedies available. The book defines redundancy and lists your rights; it explains how redundancy payment is calculated and what can be done when an employer does not pay up. It also suggests how an employer can help a redundant employee find another job.

The book deals with job hunting, how to apply, what to do to get an interview and making sure that the interview goes well. The book deals with the points to consider when being offered a job, the legal rights and obligations on both sides, and what is involved as an employee.

Living with stress

helps the reader to identify the sources of stress in his own life – following a bereavement, in a job or in unemployment, in marriage or before or after divorce, in loneliness or in overcrowding. It lists the common warning signs and indicates what steps to take in order to adapt successfully or change what needs to be changed.

The book looks at the physical and emotional harm that can result if stress is not kept under control and unnecessary stress eliminated. It outlines the right and wrong ways to counteract stress – from smoking, drinking and drugs to a whole range of beneficial attitudes and activities.

On getting divorced

explains the grounds for divorce in England and Wales and describes the procedure for an undefended divorce without a court hearing. It goes on to deal in detail with the practical arrangements that have to be made, about the home, the children, finances, and how problems are settled by the court. Tax, national insurance and help from the state welfare services and voluntary organisations are also covered.

Avoiding heart trouble

identifies the factors which make a person more likely to develop heart trouble and describes how the various risk factors interact; cigarette smoking, raised blood pressure, high level of blood fats, stress, hereditary and dietary factors, oral contraceptives, overweight. It warns of the more serious signs and symptoms of heart trouble and, where possible, tells you what can be done about them.

Avoiding back trouble

explains how the spine is constructed and how not to stress it in everyday activities such as housework, driving, lifting and carrying, gardening, sitting. It describes symptoms of back trouble and advises on how to cope with an acute attack of back pain. It tells what to expect when examined by specialists (including the diagnostic terms that may be used) and the treatments that may be prescribed. The book ends with suggestions about how to avoid becoming a chronic back sufferer.

Living through middle age

faces up to the changes that this stage of life may bring, whether inevitable (in skin, hair, eyes, teeth) or avoidable, such as being overweight, smoking or drinking too much, insomnia. It discusses the symptoms and treatment of specific disorders that are fairly common in men and women over 40, and for women the effects of the menopause and gynaecological problems. Psychological difficulties for both men and women are discussed, and the possible need for sexual adjustment. Throughout, practical advice is given on overcoming problems that may arise.

Dealing with household emergencies

is written for the un-handy householder who needs basic facts about simple action to take when a sudden emergency occurs. It gives advice on electrical failure, blocked drains and pipes, broken window cords and panes, stains, outbreak of fire, infestation by pests, and has a section on first aid and on making an insurance claim after an accident or damage.

Cutting your cost of living

suggests ways of spending less money without changing your standard of living. The book includes ideas on how to reduce your bills for food, toiletries, heating and holidays. There is a section on managing your money, and practical advice is given on growing your own fruit and vegetables, and on what jobs it is worth doing yourself.

Making the most of your freezer

helps the reader to make the right choice between chest, upright, or fridge-freezer and where to keep it. What to do if things go wrong is explained in words, illustrations and yes/no flow-charts. There is also a full list of names and addresses of freezer manufacturers or importers in the UK. It describes what repairs can be carried out by the householder and when a service engineer should be called. It gives hints on food labelling and keeping a freezer record and what to do when there is a power cut, how to replace the door seal, dealing with rust, defrosting and cleaning.

The book includes a section on growing your own fruit and vegetables, with freezing in mind, and it includes in tabular form hard facts on preparation, storage time, thawing time, and suitability for freezing of meat, fish, bread, cakes and pastry, dairy products, fruit and vegetables.

Where to live after retirement

tackles the difficult subject of a suitable place to live in old age. The book offers practical advice on the decision whether to move or to stay put and adapt the present home to be easier to live in. It weighs up the pros and cons of the alternatives open to an older person, and the financial aspects involved, considers sheltered housing and granny flats, the problems of living in someone else's household, and residential homes.

Raising the money to buy your home

gives detailed information about the requirements of the various lenders –
building society, bank, local authority, insurance company, private lender
– and the procedures involved. It explains the importance of the timing of
a loan and what to do when ending a mortgage early. Simple examples
show how to work out what your own financial commitments are going to
be throughout the period of the loan and how to use a simple calculator to
work out the amount of loan outstanding at any time and, when interest
rates change, what your monthly payments will be.

Which? way to buy, sell and move house

takes you through all the stages of moving to another home – considering
the pros and cons of different places, house hunting, viewing, having a
survey, making an offer, getting a mortgage, completing the purchase,
selling the present home. It explains the legal procedures and the likely
costs. Buying and selling at an auction and in Scotland are specifically dealt
with. The practical arrangements for the move and for any repairs or
improvements to the new house are described. Advice is given for easing
the tasks of sorting, packing and moving possessions, people and pets,
with a removal firm or by doing it yourself, and for making the day of the
move go smoothly.

The legal side of buying a house

covers the procedure for buying an owner-occupied house with a registered
title in England or Wales (not Scotland) and describes the part played by
the solicitors and building society, the estate agent, surveyor, Land Registry, insurance company and local authority. It takes the reader step by step
through a typical house purchase so that, in many cases, he can do his own
conveyancing without a solicitor; it also deals with the legal side of selling.

Central heating

helps you to choose central heating for your home, giving details of the
equipment involved – boilers, radiators, heat emitters, thermostats and
other controls, warm air units, ducting – and discussing the different fuels,
the importance of insulation, and the installation.

Securing your home

should help you keep burglars and car thieves at bay by telling you how to protect your home and safeguard your car. It gives practical advice on making it difficult for the burglar to get in; locks and grilles, burglar alarms, and general safety are all dealt with. And it tells you what to do and what not to do if a burglar has broken into your home or car, and how to make a claim on your insurance.

Pregnancy month by month

tells in detail what a pregnant woman can expect at each stage of antenatal care. The book discusses where to have a baby, and compares hospital, GP maternity unit, nursing home and home confinement. It gives reasons for the various tests and examinations at antenatal clinics, and tells how to deal with the minor ailments that often accompany pregnancy. Sections on genetic counselling, having twins, claiming maternity benefits, fertility problems, contraception, abortion and provisions for unmarried mothers are also included.

The newborn baby

deals primarily with the first weeks after the baby is born, with information about feeding and development in the following weeks and months. The daily routines, such as feeding, bathing, nappy changing, sleeping, are covered and the book tells how to identify and cope with minor upsets that may cause alarm but are normal and also the more serious ailments that should be reported to the doctor. The book also deals with routine matters such as immunization, tests, visits to the clinic.

Which? way to slim

is the complete guide to losing weight and staying slim. The book separates fact from fallacy, and gives a balanced view of essentials such as suitable weight ranges, target weights, exercise, and the advantages and disadvantages of different methods of dieting. The book highlights the dangers of being overweight and warns of the risks in middle age, during pregnancy, when giving up smoking. Every aspect of slimming is appraised – from appetite suppressants to yoga.

There are also sections on slimmers' cookery, foods and aids for slimmers, eating out, slimming groups, help from doctors, the psychology of slimming, activity and exercise. Tables of Calorie and carbohydrate values of foods and drinks are provided for easy day-to-day reference.

Which? 25 years on

gives a panoramic view of the first twentyfive years of *Which?* and traces the development of the Consumers' Association, recording not only the triumphs and progress that have made *Which?* the power it is today, but also the set-backs and opposition that had to be overcome.

The book is the personal view of Eirlys Roberts, for many years the editor and moving spirit of *Which?*. It examines the influences on the creation of *Which?* and describes how a variety of diverse strands came together in the late 1950's that made possible the consumer movement.

This illustrated book is a special publication to mark the Consumers' Association's silver jubilee in 1982.

Consumer Publications are available from Consumers' Association, Caxton Hill, Hertford SG13 7LZ and from booksellers.